Tova's Garden

I would like to receive advance notice about future Tova's Garden© books, the quarterly newsletter and other information for Intermountain and High Desert Gardening. Please add me to the mailing list. ☐

Yes, I would like to order additional books.

	Price	No. of books	Amount
Perennials	$14.95	_____	_____
Mr. Vegetable	$14.95	_____	_____
	Sub Total		_____
	7% Sales Tax (NV only)		_____
	Shipping & Handling		_____
	Total		_____

Shipping: $4.00 for the first book, add $2.00 for each additional book.

I understand that I may return any books for a full refund-- for any reason, no questions asked.

||||||BARCODE|||||| MW00637755
or fax to (702) 322-3022

Name _____

Address _____

City/State/Zip _____

Tel. Number (____) _____

Fax Number (____) _____

Check Enclosed ☐

Method of Payment   Visa ☐   M/C ☐

Card Number _____

Expiration Date _____

Signature _____

DO YOU HAVE GREAT SOIL?
GET A SOIL TEST WITHOUT LEAVING HOME

Garden soil is a dynamic ecosystem in miniature. It is teeming with plant friendly soil microbes, atmospheric gases, water and many essential plant nutrients and micronutrients. When all these are in balance, you have the foundation for growing healthy plants. Remember, plants will only be as healthy as the soil they are growing in. How do you know if you're building the right foundation to support all the hard work you're doing? Find out with this simple, easy test. Send in the coupon below, along with $19.95 (isn't that "dirt cheap?") to receive your complete Soil Testing Kit and complete instructions. Return the entire Kit via parcel post. Receive our recommendations to create the perfect environment for your garden!

Yes, Please send me my Soil Test Kit

Name _____

Address _____

City/State/Zip _____   **Phone Number (____)** _____

Payment: ☐ **Visa**   ☐ **Mastercard**   ☐ **Check/Money Order**

Card Number _____   **Expir. Date** _____

Signature _____

This book is dedicated to my husband, Barry Roseman,
who continues to be the love of my life.

"*W*here would we be if humanity had never known flowers? If they
didn't exist and had always been hidden from view....our character, our morals,
our aptitude for beauty, for happiness would they be the same?"

Maurice Maeterlinck (1862-1949)

Secrets to Success with Intermountain and High Desert
PERENNIALS

by
Tova Roseman

Debby – Make it green! Tova

First Edition 1998

ACKNOWLEDGMENTS

The author wishes to thank the following individuals for their kind cooperation in providing information, encouragement and advice throughout the preparation of this book.
Margaret Oliver, Tauni Clark, Greta Mestre, Cheryl Kinder, Catherine Hancock,
Linda Good, Dave Stipech, Tim Oriard,
Gene Klump, Pearl Berryhill, and Janet Dutt

The author also wishes to thank the staff for their research, assistance, kind comments and their writing and production of this book. Jean Bratcher, Laura McCalister and Brian Buckley.

Book design, layout, and typesetting: Roseman Marketing, Inc.
Drawings: Brian Buckley
Color separations and printing: P. Chan & Edward, Inc.

PHOTO CREDITS
Names of photographers are followed by the page numbers on which their work appears. T = top, B = bottom, L = left, R = right, C = Center, I = inset.

Richard Bissett: 26-TI, 35-TR, 56-T

Fred Cornelius: 13, 20, 21-T, 21-B, 26-B, 28, 29, 30, 32-B, 39, 47, 48, 49-TI, 51-B, 54, 55, 56-B, 66-TI, 67-T, 69-B, 71-B, 76-T, 78-B, 80, 87-B

Nancy Degenkolb: 22-B, 24-B, 35-TL, 35-TC, 35-B, 40, 41-B, 57-B, 58-T, 72-B

Jack Fleming: 48-T, 59-T, 61-T, 63-T, 66-B

John Frett: 25-T, 34, 36-T, 41-T, 42-R, 43, 45-B, 58-B, 59-B, 62-T, 67-B, 70-B, 76-B, 90-T

Catherine Hancock: 22-T, 26-T, 27-B, 38-B, 44-B, 57-T, 64, 66-T, 73, 74, 75-T, 76-TI, 77-B, 86-B, 87-T, 88-B, 89-T, 90-B, 91-B

Tova Roseman: 23, 31-B, 32-T, 33, 36-B, 38-T, 42-L, 44-T, 45-T, 46-B, 49-T, 49-B, 50-B, 51-TI, 51-BI, 52-B, 56-BI, 61-B, 63-B, 68, 71-BI, 75-B, 78-T, 79-T, 82, 83, 84, 85, 86-T, 88-T, 89-B, 91-T

Jeff Ross: 5

Bill Sonnemann: 14, 26-B, 31-T, 37, 50-T, 51-T, 69-T, 70-T, 71-T, 72-T, 77-T, 79-B, 81

Greg and Susan Speichert (Crystal Palace Perennials): 24-T, 27-T, 62-B

Collection of Strybing Arboretum Society's Helen Crocker Russell Library of Horticulture, San Francisco:
    25-B, 46-T, 52-T, 60

Notice: To the best of our knowledge the information in this book is valid. All recommendations are given without guarantees on the part of the authors and/or Roseman Marketing, Inc. The authors and/or Roseman Marketing, Inc. disclaim all liability incurred through the use of this information.

ISBN 0-943674-01-8

Roseman Publishing
Roseman Marketing, Inc.
423 W. Plumb Lane
Reno, Nevada 89509

What is Tova's Garden?

Intermountain and High Desert gardening is definitely a challenge—

poor soils, cold, wind, heat, limited rainfall and other conditions can make even the most dedicated gardener cringe. As an avid gardener who has lived in this climate for years, I've learned a lot of tips I'll share with you in this book.

You'll discover how easy it really is to:

- Design a garden that blooms for almost 9 months of the year.
- Create great soil.
- Identify and grow plants you thought wouldn't grow here.
- Create microclimates to grow what you want, where you want.
- Conserve water and still give your flowers exactly what they need with my new drip irrigation design.

My yard is the envy of my neighbors although I don't have much time to spend working on it. Many of you don't either. I wrote this book with that in mind. You'll learn the details of how to properly and easily prepare good soil, how to prune and when, how to lay out a drip system that delivers the water right to the roots of the plants and conserves water, and how and when to propagate to share your good fortune and your favorites with your friends.

You'll find an abundance of plants really do grow easily here!

Welcome to my garden and enjoy!

FOREWORD

By Dick Tracy

Garden writer, Sacramento Bee's "California Life" magazine

As a child growing up in Reno, a ritual for Mother's Day was for my younger brother and me to pitch in money we'd earned from selling newspapers after school to buy mom a flat of pansies.

Winter had shrugged off its white mantle and the bare earth in our raised planting beds begged for color. Mom was delighted and all of us would take part in planting of the flowers.

And then, usually within a week, jealous Mother Nature would level them with a hard freeze. It took three years to get the message, which was delivered by the usually non-communicative woman who lived next door: "You know you're wasting your time and money planting them now. Those flowers are going to freeze!"

My feeling was one of having been betrayed. Then why was the nursery selling them? Couldn't they tell we were kids who didn't know any better? Shouldn't they have told us to cover them with something at night?

We were transplanted New Yorkers, and there my first gardening experience had been to scatter a packet of zinnia seeds (which I found along the road walking home from school) next to our doorstep. I covered them with a little soil and forgot about them. Even I was amazed when they grew and produced a rainbow of flower heads.

Trust me, that wouldn't have happened in high-elevation Reno.

Later on in our gardening adventures (which I participated in with some reluctance, viewing horticulture as something boys should not be subjected to) dad ordered "topsoil" from a landscape contractor who lived a few doors away. His son and I were in the same grade in school and we were assured we'd get the best topsoil available.

It looked beautiful and rich, coming off the dump truck, but in truth was nothing more than sand from the desert. And when it mixed with our native clay produced a surface hard enough to dribble a basketball on. The feeble lawn that grew in the "topsoil" was less appealing to look at than the collection of green weeds we'd been mowing up to that time.,

"Compost." said the next door neighbor in disgust, "You've got to mix compost in with that topsoil if you expect anything to grow!"

It's too bad that we had no guide comparable to "Tova's Garden" in those days. It would have made life much simpler than learning through "The School of Hard Knocks" as we did.

Here's a comprehensive and easy-to-understand guide on all aspects of high desert and intermountain gardening with information presented in a friendly fashion, rather than the caustic after-the-fact comments of our next door neighbor.

Importantly too, Tova deals with microclimates that allow you to broaden (or restrict) gardening activities. Too often, books will state matter-of-factly that you can't grow things like fuchsias in your climate and you look over the fence and see them on your neighbor's patio.

We weren't lucky enough to have a gardener like Tova Roseman living next door, but you now hold all her gardening knowledge of this particular climate in your hands. In my role as a garden writer for The Sacramento Bee's "California Life" magazine, I see dozens of new gardening books during the course of a year, and I can think of none that are more straightforward, encouraging and easy to understand than this.

INTRODUCTION

Contents

Perennials are incredible garden staples. They enhance, emphasize and they consistently perform in our gardens in the high desert, intermountain regions. These beautiful plants keep expanding and spreading every year, filling up vacant space. They don't need too much extra attention once they're planted. It's also great fun to be able to divide clumps of favored perennials and share them with friends.

Many perennials last for generations. Peonies are greatly treasured in China and many plants have been passed down through families for centuries! My plants aren't that old, but I do have some from my grandmother that were originally brought to the West via wagon train. Some of these old-time favorites include peonies, iris, columbine, clematis and bleeding hearts.

In a nutshell, perennials are an easy way to develop an absolutely lush garden. In one season your yard will look great. In three years, it will be incredible!

WHAT CONSTITUTES A PERENNIAL?

Perennials are herbaceous plants that return year after year. Their stems are soft and fleshy, and in this book, include some ornamental grasses. They do not include bulbs.

The tops of perennials die down, sometimes soon after bloom, sometimes at the end of summer when cold temperatures cause them to go dormant and the green tops die down to the soil. The herbaceous stems provide food for the roots that remain alive beneath the soil in a dormant state throughout the winter. Then the warming of the soil in spring causes the end of the dormancy.

Some of the earliest blooming plants start growing as soon as the soil receives any warmth at all and actually thrive in the temperature fluctuations of spring. Once temperatures rise and become too warm, these plants complete the bloom cycle and the leaves and stems may die back to the ground. These earliest plants include peonies, bleeding hearts and oriental poppies. These perennials are followed by beautiful bloomers such as bearded iris, bee balm, delphiniums and daylilies. All perennials start to break dormancy when the ground is consistently warm although some may not bloom until summer or fall.

Biennials, sometimes mistaken for perennials, take two years to complete the life cycle. When grown from seed, they produce leaves but no flowers the first year; the second year they flower, set seed and die.

Annuals grow from seed in the spring, flower profusely throughout the summer, then die with the first hard frosts of winter, completing their entire life cycle within one year or less. Oftentimes, seeds from annuals can be left on the ground throughout the winter and they will reseed themselves in the spring.

MICROCLIMATES

Many of you are familiar with the USDA Plant Hardiness Zone Map seen in virtually every gardening catalog. The USDA map is a guide only for cold temperatures.

Now, we have a new map that has just been released–the AHS Plant Heat-Zone Map. It provides a zone guide for heat temperatures; Sunset has also recently expanded their original climate zone map from 24 to over 50 zones. What does all this mean and why all the changes? Microclimates!

In the large scope of gardening there are two all encompassing types of microclimates–urban and vegetative.

Urban Microclimates refer to what happens when cities are developed. Concrete and paving abounds, large buildings are built close together, houses spring up *en masse* and air pollution develops. Heat and wind patterns change. As you move toward the city center, temperatures increase, street corners and alleys become wind tunnels.

As you travel away from the city center the **Vegetative Microclimate** comes into play. You'll see more trees, greenery and water. Temperatures decrease and humidity increases. Microclimates are also affected by locations near the base of mountains, the direction you face, elevation, slope, prevailing winds, type of water—either running water such as a stream, or a still body of water such as a pond or lake, and so on. There could be one microclimate in the area immediately surrounding your home and a totally different microclimate right across the street.

Creating a variety of microclimates within your own yard can be as simple as re-positioning trees, shrubs and rocks, building berms, the placement of your house, adding more grass . . . the list is endless. The following diagram shows several ways to create a microclimate in your yard.

Use all of the zone maps as a guide and as a reference to expand your plant horizons, not as a limit to what you can grow. The fun of gardening is no boundaries and no rules, only information to expand upon. In your garden you can do anything you want. Try new plants that may be common in other locations within the same zone, but uncommon in your area. That's how we get new plants! What's more fun than creating a microclimate in your own yard and successfully adapting these wonderful "new" plants to your area?

Your garden is a reflection of you and it can change constantly—just like your life.

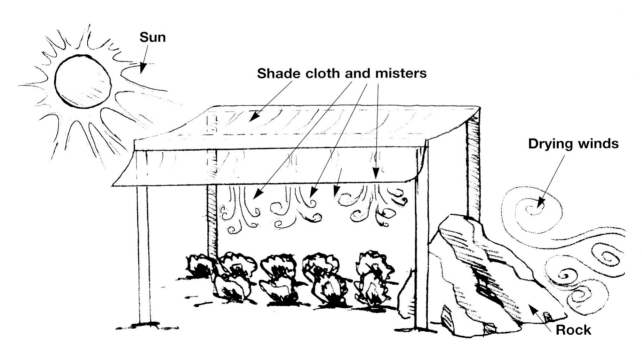

Plant some trees to develop a microclimate for shade loving plants. Then use a 40% or 60% shade cloth for the plants until the tree canopy develops.

Misters let you grow plants that require higher humidity. Rocks and berms protect plants from the hot sun and drying winds, especially during hot summer afternoons.

PLAN FOR THE LONG TERM

The key to building a healthy perennial garden is from the ground up. Healthy soil is a strong foundation that will support the lush, healthy, beautiful garden that will give you immense pleasure for many years to come.

Make your soil an excellent growing medium BEFORE you plant anything! Then you won't have to think about it for a long time. Trying to grow perennials in poor soil conditions can become frustrating and takes the fun out of a garden that doesn't perform "like the catalogs."

Lime or gypsum sweetens the soil. Use as an amendment to increase the calicum and make the soil more neutral or to reduce salinity.

KNOW YOUR SOIL

Start with a professional soil test. Grid your entire yard into at least four sectors and have each one tested individually. Tests are inexpensive, and most yards have varying types of soil—anywhere from extremely sandy to extreme clay. You'll want to make slightly different amendments for each area.

Test results will give you a guide to what type of soil amendments should be added for good plant growth. Minimum testing should include pH, nitrogen, phosphorus, potassium, salinity and organic content. More detailed tests can provide you with the availability of micronutrients such as calcium, magnesium, sulfur, iron, copper, boron, and others.

Use the coupon in the front of this book to send in your soil sample right from home.

Soil Testing

Plants can vary quite a bit regarding their needs for nutrients and soil pH. The only way I know of to determine what's in your soil is to test it. Collecting the soil for your soil test is simple. Use a trowel to recover small amounts of soil at a depth of about six inches. Take several samples from different areas across the area to be tested. Mix these together in a bucket to get an accurate indication of average soil conditions. Dry two or three handfuls of soil from the bucket at room temperature. Then place the soil in a tightly sealed container and send it to a soil testing laboratory (or use the handy-dandy soil test coupon at the front of this book).

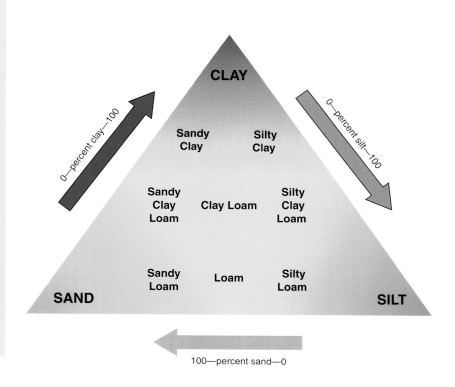

HEALTHY SOIL GIVES YOU HEALTHY PLANTS

Healthy soil provides the foundation to grow healthy plants, and healthy plants are less prone to disease and insect attacks. They can also withstand normal plant stresses more easily.

Balance is the key to soil improvement. Perennials do not like extremes in watering, soil amendments or fertilizers. Too much nitrogen causes lush vegetative growth, too little phosphorus and potassium cause your plants to produce fewer flowers and a less extensive root system.

TEXTURE AND STRUCTURE

Our soils tend to be different in the intermountain, high desert regions. They are mostly clay or mostly sand and due to limited amounts of rain, organic matter does not decay easily to provide added nutrients. For example, in other regions of the country, balled and burlapped trees are planted, burlap and all. This is done with the idea that the burlap will break down quickly in the soil moisture, adding more organic material, allowing the tree roots to grow out into the native soil. However, in our region, the burlap left surrounding a tree's roots does not decay and will actually constrict root growth.

It's extremely important to evaluate your soil and make the proper adjustments for your soil type before planting a perennial garden. Also, be prepared to incorporate certain amendments and organic materials each year to maintain good texture and structure. You'll be rewarded with the garden of your dreams--one that will perform well for you year after year.

Sandy soils allow easy root penetration and usually provide enough oxygen and carbon dioxide for the roots, but often drain too fast, depriving the roots of substantial moisture and leaching away important nutrients.

Clay soils tend to compact tightly which makes root penetration difficult, and hold too much water, preventing sufficient oxygen from reaching the roots, and drowning the plants.

Organic matter is the solution for either soil type. Add lots of it and make sure it is well broken down before you incorporate it into the soil! Organic matter increases water and nutrient holding capacity to sandy soil; breaks up clay soil making it more friable (crumbly) and allows for better drainage which helps the roots "breathe". Organic matter also
- provides a slow release of nitrogen as it decays.
- helps balance pH.
- acts as a sponge for holding water without drowning roots.
- acts as a life support medium for an entire host of soil-dwelling organisms, including soil bacteria, earthworms, and fungal hyphae that help support a healthy root system.

Plenty of organic matter
- makes your garden easier to weed and cultivate and
- conserves water.

Compost, aged manures (if not too salty), and leaf mold are examples of excellent organic soil amendments.

If you don't want to re-build really difficult soil, then you might want to consider building raised beds and fill the beds with good soil, such as a "triple mix" to start with, then mix in additional organic matter. Triple mixes vary, but generally contain a combination of top soil, compost and manure and are available at many rock and garden centers.

WHAT DO THOSE NUMBERS ON THE FERTILIZER BAGS MEAN?

16-16-16 is an example of equal parts of nitrogen, phosphorus and potassium.

Soil

Nitrogen, the first number, affects the green, vegetative body of the plant. Too little nitrogen can cause poor plant growth and reduce crop yields. Too much nitrogen may give you big, lush plants, but few fruits or flowers. Additionally, plants are more susceptible to disease and insect problems when fed too much nitrogen.

Phosphorus, the second number, is very important for the overall health of plants. Too little phosphorus causes plants and roots to be stunted. Soils in many parts of zones 5, 6 and 7 are often deficient in phosphorus. Since phosphorus does not move freely throughout the soil, it is often unavailable to the root system and small or shallow-rooted plants often feel the pinch first. An over-application of phosphorus can upset your soil chemistry balance for a long time, so be careful not to overfertilize with this nutrient. It does not leach out of the soil.

Potassium, the third number, helps plants resist disease, strengthens their stalks and improves the quality and quantity of the flowers, seeds and fruits. A lack of potassium often causes older leaves to have a "burned" look and plants may exhibit stunted growth and poor quality flowers. Sandy soils with too little organic matter are first candidates for potassium deficiency and the effects are often aggravated by dry weather.

Consider using slow-release fertilizers and amendments, well worked into the plant's root zone, so these important plant nutrients become available over an extended period of time.

Epsom salts are a good, inexpensive source of magnesium sulfate. It gives all flowering plants rich, green foliage and beautiful blooms. Add 1/8 tsp. per 1/2 gallon water to potted plants once a month. Add 1 T. per 2 gallons water once a month to the plant base of bedded plants.

pH is a measure of the soil's acidity or alkalinity. 7.0 is neutral, anything less than 7.0 becomes more acidic. Anything above 7.0 becomes more alkaline .

Alkaline soils can cause important micronutrients to become chemically "tied up" and consequently are unavailable to your plants, even if an abundance of those nutrients are available in the soil. Iron chlorosis (new leaves turning yellow in between the veins) is a common example.

Soil that is too acidic can be just as problematic. Phosphorus can become "tied up" and heavy metals such as aluminum may become too available and become toxic. Too much acid in the soil can also be irritating and even damaging to the plant's delicate root system.

Salinity is a measure of the water soluble salts in the soil. Excessive salts can harm roots directly and also cause poor plant growth by interfering with the natural osmotic uptake of water by the roots. Salinity is frequently a problem in more arid regions because the low levels of rainfall are insufficient to leach the salts out of the root zone.

Many gardeners add animal manure as a soil amendment, but sometimes manure can be high in salt. Be sure to use aged or composted manure and incorporate other types of compost for a balanced soil.

CHOOSE PERENNIALS FOR THE SOIL

You can choose from a wide variety of perennials that prefer a certain pH range, or you can adjust the pH to accommodate the perennials you prefer. The best overall pH for a majority of perennials is right in the middle, between 6.0 and 7.0, where soil nutrients are easily available to the roots.

Elemental sulfur makes soil more acid.

FERTILIZATION SECRETS

There are several options available to increase the fertility of your soil. Organic options include amendments such as alfalfa meal, blood meal, fish meal, various composts, cottonseed meal, earthworm castings, and animal manures. If you choose organic nutrients you must be aware that these materials supply less nitrogen, phosphorus and potassium than chemical fertilizers. They also release the nutrients more slowly. They do, however improve soil structure and drainage.

It's always best to properly amend your soil with compost and other organic matter. From time to time, however, adding chemical fertilizers, will give your plants an additional boost of nutrients and micronutrients they may not be getting from the soil. This is particularly true when establishing a new perennial garden. Once established, the herbaceous plant stems and leaves will provide a great deal of the nutrients perennials need to bloom year after year.

In a new garden, I find regular fertilization is most difficult because of my hectic schedule. Due to the short growing season in our zone, I try to fertilize approximately every two weeks using a water soluble fertilizer. I found I can save time and fertilize large areas quickly by lightly scattering handfuls of fertilizer over the entire planted area, rather than dissolving it first in a watering can and then watering it in. Water must be applied immediately after fertilizing to thoroughly dissolve the crystals. I'm careful to scatter it only on the soil, not on the leaves of the plants.

Twice during the growing season, I will alternate the water soluble fertilizer with a timed–release granular fertilizer which breaks down gradually over the season to provide a steady supply of nutrients.

In an established perennial bed, I prefer using a timed-release granular fertilizer for most of the growing season and only applying the water soluble fertilizer for an extra boost.

Perennials bloom better with some additional micronutrients that our soils may be lacking. Several times throughout the summer, I sprinkle a tablespoon or two of Epsom salt around the dripline of the plant, then water in. Epsom salt is a good source of magnesium sulfate. This is one secret that gives all flowering plants, including roses, rich green foliage, beautiful bloom color and lots of new growth. Epsom salt is inexpensive and can be found in any drug store.

A second secret nutrient comes from alfalfa leaves which add triacontanol to the soil. It stimulates an increase in the number of new shoots and produces more vigorous plants. Alfalfa leaves are available in feed stores and pet shops in pellet or cube form. Use only alfalfa that has not been mixed with molasses or other additives.

Use alfalfa leaves to create more vigorous plants. Alfalfa leaves increase bloom size and color.

WATERING

The new drip systems are wonderful for both you and your garden! These systems conserve water while providing exact amounts of water directly to the roots. As communities limit watering to two or three days a week, deep watering becomes essential. It's best to provide water at intervals throughout the day. The soil can absorb the water without becoming too saturated at one time which causes water to run off. Timers can be added and set to start and stop watering multiple times throughout the day automatically.

Drip lines can be placed right where the plants need them to make watering very easy. Take advantage too, of the new attachments that hold water soluble or liquid fertilizer and dispense it automatically throughout the entire drip system.

Don't make the mistake of placing only one emitter per plant. One emitter per plant provides minimal water in the soil and only to one small area, rather than to the plant's entire root system. This creates a shallow, minimal root system and ultimately, unhealthy plants that can't survive the heat of the summer or the winds throughout the season.

Follow the diagram below and you'll be thrilled with the results. I use this design for all my plants, including shrubs and trees, to produce tremendous growth and constant bloom! Plant roots need to grow and spread throughout the soil so they can absorb enough nutrients to produce beautiful, healthy, long-blooming perennials.

Banana peels are excellent for providing blooming nutrients to perennials. Since our zone doesn't compost things quickly due to drier soil conditions, shred your banana peels and bury near the roots of your flowering plants. As they decompose they provide calcium, magnesium, sulfur and phosphates.

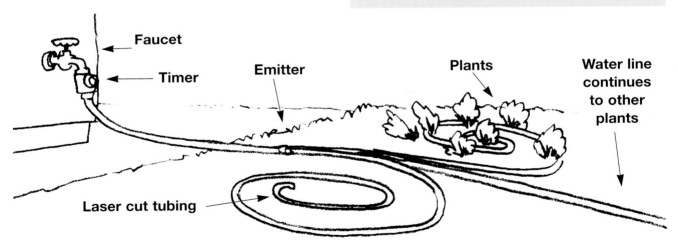

Faucet

Timer

Emitter

Plants

Water line continues to other plants

Laser cut tubing

Use either 3/4" or 1" main line, depending upon your water pressure, attached to either a hose bib or valves. Attach lengths of 1/4" microline soaker hose (microline comes with holes spaced at either 6" or 12" intervals) at varying intervals and lay out in a spiral pattern with approximately 3" spacing between spirals. Plug ends and hold spirals down with stakes as needed. Plant perennials between spirals of soaker hose.

BAREROOT PERENNIALS

Unwrap the plant gently and discard all packing materials that came with it. Dig a hole a little wider than the spread of the roots and deep enough to allow you to set the crown (the point where the leaves or stems of the plant meet the roots) approximately one inch below the surface of the soil (follow enclosed planting instructions for specific plant requirements). Make a little mound in the center of the hole, placing the plant at the center of the mound and gently spread the roots evenly over the mound. Place soil over the roots and gently firm the soil over the crown. Water thoroughly to remove air pockets and settle the soil around the roots.

CONTAINER GROWN PERENNIALS

Often plants become root-bound within the containers or pony paks. Prior to planting, moisten the plant thoroughly by placing the plant and the container in a bucket of water for a couple of hours. Then pop the plant out of the container and loosen the roots by breaking up the sides. If the roots are circling the bottom, pull apart so they are loose and can spread. This allows the roots to grow out into the surrounding soil. If the roots are severely compacted, gently cut with your trowel and break apart so they are loose enough to spread. Cutting compacted roots encourages them to

form new roots that will quickly spread into the surrounding soil and becoming established more quickly.

WATERING NEWLY PLANTED PERENNIALS

Be sure to water daily, or even several times a day if the temperatures are hot or there is wind. It takes a few weeks for plants to become established into the surrounding soil. When perennials are first planted, think of them as still being in a container, which they are, only without the pot. The small amount of soil they come with dries out quickly and until the roots spread into the surrounding soil, they will need a bit more care.

Use coffee grounds to make soil more acid.

DISEASE AND PEST CONTROL

Perennials, for the most part, are relatively disease and pest free. To reduce any possibility of problems, practice good garden maintenance and cleanliness. From time to time during the season, it helps to "clean" the garden with a mixture of 1 part inexpensive liquid dishwashing soap to 6 parts water. Spray with your garden sprayer early in the spring and then about once a month. This mixture helps remove any overwintering pests and cleans the plant leaves from smog residue, allowing them to "breathe" better.

Also consider incorporating ladybugs and praying mantis. As natural predators, they do a great job most of the time. For extra help you can use *Bacillus thuringiensis* or insecticidal soap. You may have to resort to a chemical insecticide at least once or twice throughout the season. Check your local garden store for their recommendations.

Wood ashes are a good source of potassium. They also increase pH. Wood ashes can be used in place of lime, and in equal quantities. They are low in calcium however, compared to limestone, so supplemental gypsum will be needed if the calcium level in the soil is low. Add about one or two pounds of gypsum per 100 square feet if needed. DO NOT USE fresh ashes, as they can be caustic and do not spread directly over the roots of plants or young seedlings.

MULCHING

Mulch is an essential part of any successful garden. It helps retain moisture and properly applied, mulch will also help control soil temperature, keep weeds down, prevent dirt from splashing on foliage and help control soil erosion.

Mulches are of two types, organic and inorganic. Organic mulches include materials that are naturally derived, such as cottonseed hulls, pine needles, shredded leaves, gravel or grass clippings. Inorganic mulches are materials such as black or clear plastic, or landscape fabric. Inorganics may not be the best choice for a perennial garden as they eliminate volunteers and makes plant division difficult.

Organic mulches look great and add nutrients to the soil. Once mulches are broken down by soil organisms, earthworms and weather, your soil will become that rich, dark humus that helps your perennials really thrive! Mulches such as pine needles can also be used as soil amendments. If your pH test indicated your soil was alkaline, pine needles can be used to acidify the soil.

To apply an organic mulch, prepare the area by pulling any weeds, till and water the area thoroughly. Spread in sections, two to three inches of mulch directly over the soil. Do not pack the mulch against the stems of your plants. Allow some "breathing room" by leaving a few inches of space. Mulches tend to settle, so fluff the mulch from time to time with either your hands or lightly with a rake to maintain air circulation.

If you're going to use an inorganic mulch, I recommend landscape fabric. It keeps down weeds while preserving soil moisture and air circulation, and if covered with an organic mulch such as shredded bark, the nutrients from the bark will flow through to the soil with the water.

WINTER PROTECTION

Toward the end of summer, around mid-August, it's best to stop fertilizing and cut back on watering. It's time to start preparing for the onset of winter. The goal is to deter any new plant growth and instead encourage the perennials to put all their energy into food storage. If we're lucky enough to experience that beautiful Indian Summer as we often do in this zone, your perennials will have a wonderfully long period to prepare for the tumultuous temperature fluctuations coming up.

Since we don't experience long, wet winter periods where left over plant material decays and becomes a holding place for insects, I prefer to let my plants go through the autumn and winter months without pruning. The dead leaves and stalks act as a natural protective mulch, providing air circulation and preventing snow and water from packing in around the main plant stem.

After the ground freezes, you can place straw or shredded newspaper lightly covering your more delicate perennials. If you've used an organic mulch, simply rake it over the plants.

Now you can enjoy a cozy winter yourself, feeling confident that your plants are well protected.

The diagram to the right illustrates how to prune iris. Once the bloom period is complete, trim the leaves and flower stalk into a fan-shape no less than six inches tall. The remaining leaves will then provide nutrients to the rhizomes for excellent bloom the following year.

PRUNING

For pruning of perennnials in general, I recommend pruning to shape, rejuvenate plants or to remove dead plant stalks.

To rejuvenate a plant, it helps to hard-prune, almost back to the ground. It forces it to produce a lot of new, soft growth, sending out new buds and shoots. Hard pruning should only be done in the spring, after all danger of frost has passed. Prune throughout the growing season to shape or remove dead plant parts. DO NOT prune when the summer temperatures get hot. Leave all clean-up until the spring, rather than in the fall. If you must have a spotless yard, this will drive you crazy, but it is necessary to provide a protective mulch over the winter. As the plants die back, the dead matter from the top protects and insulates the roots against our drying winds, cold dry air and temperature fluctuations throughout the winter. The diagram below illustrates how to prune iris. Once the bloom period is complete, trim the leaves and flower stalk into a fan-shape no less than six inches tall. The remaining leaves will then provide nutrients to the rhizomes for excellent bloom the following year.

HEAT AND HARDINESS ZONE MAPS
How to tell at a glance if your plants will be happy in the High Desert and Intermountain Region

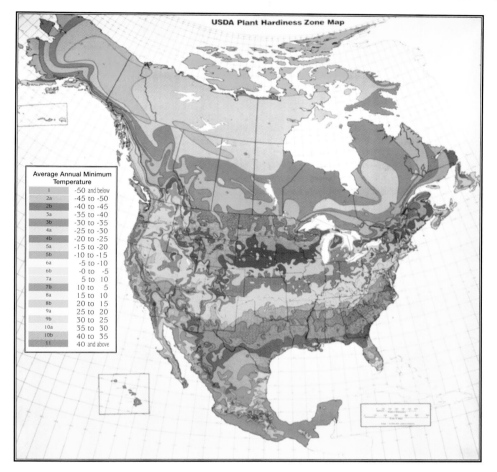

USDA Plant Hardiness Zone Map

Average Annual Minimum Temperature	
1	-50 and below
2a	-45 to -50
2b	-40 to -45
3a	-35 to -40
3b	-30 to -35
4a	-25 to -30
4b	-20 to -25
5a	-15 to -20
5b	-10 to -15
6a	-5 to -10
6b	-0 to -5
7a	5 to 10
7b	10 to 5
8a	15 to 10
8b	20 to 15
9a	25 to 20
9b	30 to 25
10a	35 to 30
10b	40 to 35
11	40 and above

Use both maps to check out both heat and cold tolerance of any new plants you wish to purchase. While many plants need a certain amount of chilling and dormancy to perform and bloom their best, perennials also need shifts in both temperature and daylength over a year's period to bloom well.

The USDA Plant Hardiness Zone Map provides a guide to the winter and summer hardiness of the plant varieties you are thinking of using (example: Zones 5-7 indicate the northern and southern extremes for the plant). Many nurseries and catalogs use these codes to help you make good decisions.

Don't forget, the soil content, moisture, sun/shade, and microclimate can affect any plant's performance for good or ill. It's a good idea to look over your neighbor's fence and see what's working, and oh, read this book!

The American Horticulture Society Plant-Heat Zone Map

has just been released and is the newest information on plant heat tolerance. It takes the idea of the Hardiness Zone Map one step further, indicating the average number of days above 86°. The highest number on the container or listing will show you the southernmost zone in which the plant will thrive if you give it the ordinary care it requires.

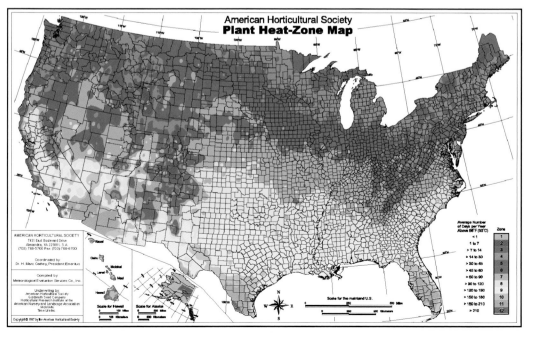

American Horticultural Society **Plant Heat-Zone Map**

Average Number of Days per Year Above 86°F (30°C)	Zone
< 1	1
1 to 7	2
> 7 to 14	3
> 14 to 30	4
> 30 to 45	5
> 45 to 60	6
> 60 to 90	7
> 90 to 120	8
> 120 to 150	9
> 150 to 180	10
> 180 to 210	11
> 210	12

"The only limit to your garden is the boundaries of your imagination."

Thomas D. Church
American Landscaper

$\mathcal{A}$STILBE
(Astilbe spp.)

Most varieties were developed in Germany in the early 1900's and are native to Asia. Most *Astilbe* that nurseries offer are hybrids of *Astilbe x arendsii*. Excellent for cutting and used fresh or for drying.

A. chinensis pumila is a dwarf plant that grows to less than one foot tall. It's pink blooms appear in late summer and tolerate dry soils. The slowly creeping roots make it a nice ground cover.

A. simplicifolia varieties have only 6-inch tall bronze-green foliage. Flowers bloom in mid-summer on branching, arching stalks. 'Sprite' has open flower clusters with an apple-blossom pink color.

- White, pink, red or purple flower clusters of fluffy plumes on mounded green foliage. Leaves are coppery color when young.
- Prefers moist, fertile soil in shaded areas.
- Bloom time differs between varieties. Usually between late May through July.
- Height 2 to 4 feet.
- Propagate by division every three to four years.
  - *Attracts butterflies.*
  - *Deer resistant.*

$\mathcal{B}$ABY'S $\mathcal{B}$REATH
(Gypsophila paniculata)

This genus is found in the alpine regions of Central and Eastern Europe to Central Africa. Find a permanent place for *Gypsophila*. The roots do not like to be disturbed. In acidic soils, apply lime in the fall. Do not allow lime to come in contact with the roots. *G. repens* or creeping baby's breath is a low growing species. Grows 4 to 8 inches with white and lilac flowers over gray foliage.

- Tiny pink or white flowers on delicate green branches.
- Full sun or light shade, tolerates dry conditions. Will rot in soggy soils. Named cultivars are commonly grafted onto species rootstock. Plant grafts in early spring with the grafting union 1 inch below the soil.
- Blooms June to July. Shear flowers before going to seed for continuous bloom.
- Height 3 to 4 feet, depending on variety.
- Propagate by seed.

Basket of Gold, Golden Tuft
(Aurinia saxatilis or Alyssum saxatile)

This member of the mustard family is native to the Mediterranean region, Central Europe and Turkey. Basket of gold tends to sprawl in rich, moist soils but remains compact and bushy in drier soils. Good for rock gardens. It is generally hardy but may be killed in extreme winters.

- Small, bright yellow flowers bloom profusely on gray-green foliage. This plant spreads rapidly and becomes very dense.
- Full sun or partial shade. Tolerates dry, infertile conditions.
- Blooms April to May. Shear flowers lightly after bloom.
- Height 9 to 12 inches.
- Propagate by division. Seeds, however, do need some light to germinate.

Bee Balm, Sweet Bergamot
(Monarda didyma)

Monarda is a genus containing about 15 members and is native to the prairies and woodlands of North America. Like other members of the mint family, the leaves are tartly aromatic and have a variety of uses. They can be dried and used as a tea or are sometimes used to mask odors in oils and perfumes.

Named cultivars seem to grow better than species and bees seem to be most attracted to red flowered cultivars. This plant spreads vigorously in shady locations with rich soil.

- Red, pink, purple or white flowers on dark green foliage.
- Plant in consistently moist, well-drained soil.
- Blooms June to July. Blooms best in light shade. Remove faded flowers to prolong bloom. Has attractive seed heads.
- Height 2 to 3 feet.
- Propagate by division.

Attracts butterflies, hummingbirds, and bees.
Deer resistant.

BELLFLOWER
(Campanula spp.)

Bellfowers vary greatly in size and habit. *Campanula* contains about 300 species of annuals, biennials and perennials. Some of the best varieties for this zone are listed below.

CARPATHIAN BELLFLOWER, TUSSOCK BELLFLOWER, CARPATHIAN HAREBELL
(C. carpatica)

Native to Central Europe. Mulch during the drier seasons to keep roots cool. Although this variety does tolerate dry soils, it is shorter lived under these conditions.

- Delicate blue or white flowers.
- Grows best in light shade and moist soils.
- Blooms June to September. Deadhead flowers to encourage repeat blooms.
- Height 6 to 18 inches.
- Propagate by dividing clumps, or from seed.

CLUSTERED BELLFLOWER
(C. glomerata)

From Europe, Turkey and parts of Asia. Excellent cut flower that can last in a vase for up to two weeks.

- Delicate blue or deep purple densely clustered flowers. Tends to have more foliage than flowers.
- Grows best in light shade and moist soils.
- Blooms July to September.
- Height 1 to 2 feet.
- Propagate by division. Rhizomatous plant multiplies quickly in richer soils.

SERBIAN BELLFLOWER
(C. poscharskyana)

Native to mountainous areas of Bosnia, Croatia and Herzegovina. Very vigorous plant spreads via underground runners. Nice plant for trailing over dry walls.

- Star shaped, pale lavender flowers over round, mid-green leaves.
- Plant in moist, well-drained soil with full sun to part shade.
- Height 2 to 6 inches.
- Blooms June to August.
- Propagate by division.

Cut bellflowers benefit from a hot water bath immediately after cutting. Immerse angled-cut flower stems in 1 inch of boiling water for about one minute. Then plunge the entire stem, up to the flower base, into tepid (100-110° F) water and allow the flowers to soak.

BERGENIA, HEARTLEAF
(Bergenia cordifolia)

This member of the saxifrage family is native to Siberia, Mongolia and the Himalayas. Bergenia is a very adaptable, extremely hardy plant that's a good choice for the border or as a ground cover. These plants grow very slowly by rhizomes that creep along the soil surface.

- Pink, red or white flowers appearing in clusters above medium-green, fleshy foliage that tinges red in winter.
- Grows in dry or moist soils but requires shade.
- Blooms April to May. Fertilize monthly.
- Height 8 to 12 inches.
- Propagate by division or seeds.

🐰 **Rabbit resistant.**

BLEEDING HEART
(Dicentra spectabilis)

D. spectabilis is native to Japan and is the showiest of the *Dicentra* species. Try to keep plants out of windy areas. Grows best in light shade. Foliage burns and dies back quickly in full sun.

Members of the *Dicentra* genus are **poisonous** to animals. The leaves, stems and roots of the plant contain a morphine-like substance which may affect cattle, horses and sheep. However, animals find *Dicentra* unpleasant and will not eat it if more palatable forage is available.

- Pink, red or white heart-shaped flowers on long, delicate branches of light green fern-like foliage.
- Requires rich, moist, well-drained, slightly acidic soil. Plant crowns will rot if left in soggy soils.
- Blooms May to June. Foliage dies down after bloom. Do not remove foliage until it turns yellow and pulls easily away from roots.
- Height 24 to 30 inches.
- Propagate by division. Plants self-sow freely in ideal conditions.

🦌 **Deer resistant.**

Little flower–but if I could understand
What you are, root and all, and all in all
I should know what God and (woman) is.

Alfred, Lord Tennyson

BUGBANE, BLACK SNAKEROOT
(Cimicifuga racemosa)

This very long lived plant is native from Massachusetts to Ontario; south to Georgia, Tennessee and Missouri. Grows tallest in deeply cultivated soils with no more than four hours of direct sunlight each day. Will not bloom in full shade. Since it prefers cooler soils, mulch deeply. Flower stalks may need staking in windier areas.

C. simplex, Autumn snakeroot 'Brunette' has brown-purple foliage with purple-tinted, off-white flowers. This plant blooms later than *C. racemosa*—in September and October.

- Tall, arching white flowers on fern-like foliage. Flowers have unusual heady fragrance.
- Plant in full sun or partial shade in average, moist, well-drained soil.
- Blooms May to July. Lateral branches may continue bloom into August.
- 2 to 3 feet foliage clumps with flowers 2 to 3 feet above.
- Propagate by division, placing rhizome so that eyes (be sure to have at least two) are precisely 1 inch below soil level.

BUTTERCUP, CREEPING
(Ranunculus repens)

This genus which contains about 400 species tolerates a range of habitats, varying from damp woodland to grassland. Creeping buttercup can be invasive. Their thick fibrous roots have runners that can grow several feet in one season.

- Double glossy, bright yellow, globe-like flowers on dark green foliage with erect stems and hairy, serrated leaves.
- Erect ground cover that grows in sun or shade.
- Blooms May to July and again in fall.
- Height 4 inches.
- Propagate by underground stolons.

Leaves and stems can be poisonous to animals if ingested.

CANDYTUFT, EVERGREEN
(Iberis sempervirens)

This Southern European native can also be called *Iberis commutata* and is nice for rock gardens. During a mild winter, plants may bloom as early as November. Will stop flowering if soil is too dry.

- Flowers white or lavender on dark green evergreen leaves. Looks good all winter.
- Grows in full sun or light shade, tolerates dry soil.
- Blooms May to June and again in September if seed pods are trimmed after first blooming.
- Height 9 to 12 inches.
- Propagate by division, seeds or cuttings.

🦋 *Attracts butterflies.* 🦌 *Deer resistant.*

COLUMBINE
(Aquilegia spp.)

This member of the buttercup family is native to the Great Basin at higher elevations. *A. canadensis* is the wildflower version of columbine that has small yellow and red flowers that can last up to six weeks on the plant.

Columbine must have perfect drainage or the plant will be short lived. Prefers moist conditions, although becomes more adaptable as it becomes established. Mulch plants from late fall to early spring. Needs protection from high winds.

Hybridizers have developed flowers from 1-1/4 to 4 inches across and up to 6 inches long.

Seed pods make interesting additions to dried flower arrangements.

If plants are hybridized, seeds will produce plants that differ from hybrid parents. Seeds need light to germinate and germinate best if chilled for 3 to 4 weeks in the refrigerator.

- Flower color red, yellow, lavender, pink. Foliage is light green with a dusty cast that catches and holds dewdrops.
- Grow in light shade or afternoon shade with a well-drained soil.
- Blooms May to June.
- Height 1 to 3 feet.
- Can propagate by division in late summer. Will self-sow in favorable conditions.

🦋 *Attracts hummingbirds and butterflies.*

🦌 *Deer resistant.*

As with all members of the buttercup family, columbine may be poisonous to animals.

CORALBELLS
(Heuchera sanguinea)

Coralbells are native to Mexico and Arizona. Provide a winter mulch in areas where continual freezing and thawing can cause heaving. Cut flowers are a nice, long-lived addition to fresh flower arrangements. When the crown gets too woody, dig up the plant, discard the woody part and replant the side shoots. Will multiply rapidly and self-sow in ideal conditions.

- Flowers pink, red or white with neat, scalloped foliage that creates a nice ground cover.
- Grows in sun or shade with rich, organic, well-drained soil. Stem rot may result in heavier soils.
- Blooms June to September and will bloom continually if deadheaded.
- Height 1 to 2 feet.
- Divide clumps when they become overcrowded, or too woody.

Attracts hummingbirds.

CREEPING PHLOX
(Phlox subulata)

Genus of about 70 species of evergreen or herbaceous, low-growing plants. *P. subulata* is an evergreen species that can also be commonly called moss pink or moss phlox and is native to Eastern and Central United States. *P. stolonifera* is another creeping phlox but is herbaceous in nature and spreads through underground stems.

Somewhat drought tolerant, prefers medium moisture. Centers tend to die out when receiving too much water and as the plants age.

- Dense, evergreen leaves forming a cushion of elliptic, bright green leaves covered with white, purple, red, lilac or pink 1 inch star-shaped flowers.
- Grows in sun or shade. Plant in sun for best bloom.
- Blooms April to June. Shearing plant after flowering keeps it compact and bushy.
- Height 2 to 6 inches.
- Propagate by seed in early spring.

The name Delphinium comes from the Greek word "Delphinion"
which means dolphin–the shape the flowers resemble.

$\mathcal{D}$ELPHINIUM
(Delphinium spp.)

This member of the Ranunculaceae family, contains three groups: Belladonna, Elatum and Pacific Hybrids. Belladonna and Elatum are perennial, while Pacific Hybrids are biennial. *Delphinium X belladonna* is a shorter species but may be longer lived and produces more spikes per plant than the Pacific Hybrids. Native to Siberia and central Europe, delphiniums are commonly referred to as larkspur although larkspur is usually classed in the genus *Consolida*.

All varieties carry varying ranges of single or double flowers on tall spikes, with a "bee" formed by inner sepals.

When planting, add some superphosphate to the bottom of the planting hole and make sure the crown is not covered. Give delphs a winter mulch. Taller varieties must be staked in windy areas of the garden or the hollow stems will break. Tend to be shorter lived in warmer climates. Do not allow foliage to get wet.

Remove all but two or three of the strongest new shoots in the spring. Set in stakes and apply a complete fertilizer around the plant. After blooming, cut the flower spikes but leave the foliage. Cut the old flower stalks to the ground after the new shoots are a few inches high. Fertilize once again in late summer to help the second blooming along. Dries nicely, hang upside down for best results. Dried flowers make a colorful addition to potpourri.

Delphinium X belladonna is not the source of the antispasmodic drug, belladonna. The drug is extracted from the plant *Atropa belladonna*.

- Colorful, elegant flower spikes above clumps of lobed medium green foliage. Colors in many shades of white, pink, blue, lavender, purple, yellow and red.
- Needs a rich, porous soil and regular fertilizing in full sun to light shade for best growth. Blend in soil conditioners for heavier, clayey soils. Add lime to excessively acidic soils.
- Blooms May to June.
- Height ranges from 2 to 5 feet. Excellent as tall accent plants.
- Propagate by seed, division or stem cuttings in early spring or late fall. Easily grown from seed.

 *Attracts hummingbirds and butterflies.*

Plant juices are known to be poisonous to cattle.

*F*ALSE *I*NDIGO
(Baptisia australis)

This member of the pea family is native from Pennsylvania south to North Carolina. False indigo got its name because it used to be grown in the southeastern United States as a substitute for indigo.

Can tolerate light shade, but it may not bloom as well. False indigo actually prefers poorer soils, and an established plant can tolerate drought. Relatively care-free plant.

Since it is a legume, it can fixate its own nitrogen. Thus, it needs little, if any, feeding. Remove spent flowers to encourage a second blooming.

The first hard frost turns the foliage a dramatic black color which make an attractive addition to dried flower arrangements.

- Foliage is bright green, and dense. Flowers are lavender to dark purple.
- Plant in light, porous soil in full sun.
- Blooms late May to early June.
- Height 3 to 4 feet.
- Propagate by seeds or division.

Attracts hummingbirds.

*F*OXTAIL *L*ILY, *D*ESERT *C*ANDLE
(Eremurus spp.)

This genus of the *Liliaceae* family has about 50 species of clump-forming, fleshy-rooted plants found in dry grassland and semi-desert areas of Asia. May require staking in wind prone areas. The leaves die back to conical crown after flowering. Dramatic in fresh floral arrangements. Cut flower spike when lowest flowers on the spike open. Needs winter chill to induce flowering. Handle the brittle roots carefully. They may rot when bruised or broken.

- Tall flower spikes of yellow, orange or salmon pink on leafless stems.
- Prefers fertile, sandy, well-drained soil in full sun to light shade.
- Height 4 to 5 feet.
- Blooms late May to early June.
- Propagate by division after flowering.

Attracts hummingbirds

$\mathcal{G}$AURA, $\mathcal{W}$HITE
(Gaura lindheimeri)

'Whirling Butterflies' is probably the most descriptive of the varieties. Native to prairies of United States. Excellent for borders and natural plantings. Deadhead spent flowers to encourage a display in fall. Deadheading also improves the plant's appearance and discourages self-seeding.

- Wispy clusters of white to rose flowers on willow-like foliage.
- Prefers rich, well-drained soil in full sun to light shade. Tolerates drought and heat.
- Bloom June to September.
- Height 3 to 4 feet.
- Propagate through seeds or division, plants self-sow readily.

$\mathcal{G}$LOBEFLOWER, $\mathcal{C}$HINESE
(Trollius chinensis)

Native to Europe and arctic North America. Can also be called *Trollius ledebourii*. Genus of about 24 species of buttercup-like, clump-forming plants. Flowers are long-lived in the vase. Remove spent flowers regularly for a second late-summer bloom. Seeds may take as long as 2 years to germinate.

- Bowl-shaped, light orange-yellow flowers with long petals (actually basal leaves) with lance-shaped lobes divided into sharply toothed segments.
- Plant in shade to part shade with a rich, peat soil or in a sunny spot with a rich, moist soil. Needs regular water.
- Blooms May to July.
- Height 3 feet.
- Propagate by seed or by division immediately after flowering.

There are many legends of the Christmas rose. One tells a story of a country girl named Madelon who visits the Christ child in Bethlehem. She is sad because she does not have a gift to bring him. An angel sees Madelon's sadness, takes her outside, and touches a wing to the ground. The first Christmas rose blooms on the spot touched by the angel. Madelon brings the Christmas rose to Bethlehem as a gift for baby Jesus.

*H*ELLEBORUS
(Ranunculaceae spp.)

The scientific name *Helleborus* derives from the Greek words "elein" meaning to injure and "bora" which means food.

In ancient times, hellebore was used as a medicinal plant that was thought to have cured mental disorders.

All species of *Helleborus* are very hardy and ranked among the most valuable of all shade plants.

Find a permanent spot for *Helleborus,* they are slow to re-establish.

CHRISTMAS ROSE
(H. niger)

Christmas rose is native to open woodlands in Southern and Central Europe, the Southern and Eastern Alps and Northern Italy. Can bloom in November depending on winter warm spells.

The Lenten rose (*H. orientalis*) is native to Turkey. Its foliage is lighter green than *H. niger*, but it is evergreen in all but the roughest of winters. Give it a mulch in the fall. This plant blooms from March to May and has very long-lived flowers. They can last up to 8 weeks.

CORSICAN HELLEBORE
(Helleborus lividus corsicus)

More adapted to mild climate regions of the Southwest, but can be grown further north if protected from drying winds.

- Clusters of green, white, pink or purple flowers over evergreen, leathery foliage.
- Prefers moist, highly organic soil.
- Blooms April to May, sometimes earlier.
- Height 12 to 18 inches.
- Propagate by seed or division.

🦌 ***Resists deer.***

The entire Christmas rose plant is poisonous to animals and humans. The powerful toxins are found particularly in the rhizomes and are not destroyed in drying or storage.

*I*CE *P*LANT, HARDY YELLOW
(Delosperma nubigenum)

This cold hardy South African succulent (comes from colder, high mountains) is the hardiest of all ice plants. Has shown hardiness to -25°F. Excellent for rock gardens. Seeds germinate best when the soil temperature is 70°F.

- Light yellow daisy-like flowers cover succulent, evergreen stems and leaves forming a vigorous carpet-like ground cover that's perfect for the windy area of the garden. Foliage turns bright red in winter.
- Full sun or partial shade.
- Blooms in June to July.
- Height 2 inches.
- Propagate with seed or by taking stem cuttings in spring or summer.

ICE PLANT, SHRUBBY
(Ruschia spp.)

Genus contains about 350 species of shrubby, almost stemless perennial succulents from the semi-desert regions of Namibia and South Africa. It has only recently been introduced to our region.

The creeping shrubby ice plant *(R. pulvinaris)* grows well in rock gardens. It blooms vigorously in late May for three to four weeks with bright, fuchsia pink, daisy-like flowers.

The trailing shrubby ice plant *(R. hamata)* is another South African native that creeps like rosemary. This plant has woody stems with small, succulent, evergreen leaves. This plant is useful in the rock garden or try allowing it to cascade over a rock wall.

- Foliage is evergreen and arranged in boat-shaped pairs. Bright fuschia-pink flowers on succulent, evergreen stems and leaves forming a tight cushion. Prolific bloomer.
- Easy to grow in fast-draining, sandy soils of average fertility. Full sun or partial shade.
- Blooms April to May and early fall.
- Height 3 inches.
- Propagate by cuttings.

Gardenmaking is creative work, just as much as painting or writing a poem. It is a personal expression of self, an individual conception of beauty.

Hanna Rion

IRIS, BEARDED
(Iris spp.)

Known for ease of growth and bloom. A good "starter" plant for first-time gardeners.

Iris flowers are made up of large, upright standards that flare to the fall of the petal. The prominent "beard" consists of white or colored hairs in the center of each fall petal.

Irises need excellent drainage as they will rot in poorly drained soils. Keep moist during active growth, water moderately after growth and keep dry during dormancy. Buds and increases occur during the post-bloom period so make sure to keep watering them for about 6 weeks after blooming. Mulch where winters are severe to prevent the rhizomes from heaving.

Many bearded irises are fragrant. Taller cultivars tend to have larger flowers and may need to be staked.

Plant and divide during July and August in cold winter areas, and in September and October where summer temperatures are high. If flowers seem smaller, the rhizomes should be divided. Dig up clumps and save the rhizomes with largest and healthiest leaves. Discard the older, leafless rhizomes from the clump's center. Also discard any rhizomes that have holes in them. The holes are usually indicative of iris borer infestation. Trim the leaves and roots to about 6 inches and allow the cut ends to heal for several hours before replanting. Amend the soil with plenty of organic matter before planting.

- Showy flowers in a wide variety of colors on spiky fans of medium green, sword-shaped leaves.
- Prefer neutral to slightly acidic soil in full sun or partial shade.
- Blooms April to May. Avoid high nitrogen fertilizer.
- Height 8 inches to 3 feet, depending on variety.
- Easily propagated by division of rhizomes.

For content iris, keep them well-fed and on the move. Transplant them in August or refresh the soil about every three years.

When planting iris, dig a hole a bit deeper than the longest roots. Then place a handful of 0-20-0 fertilizer (superphosphate) in the hole and cover with a small amount of soil. Lay the rhizome on top of the soil and cover.

Yellow iris (Iris pseudacorus) and blue flag (Iris versicolor) are poisonous if the rhizomes are ingested. The plant's sap can also cause skin rashes on sensitive people.

LADY'S MANTLE
(Alchemilla mollis)

This member of the rose family is native to Europe. *Alchemilla* is known to assist the skin's healing process. This very hardy plant can withstand -30°F temperatures.

Removing spent flowers will prevent lady's mantle's notorious spreading habit. Flowers are attractive in dried or fresh arrangements.

- Low-growing mounded plant with flowers of greenish yellow clusters on large rounded or lobed, slightly hairy, grayish green leaves.
- Needs consistent soil moisture in shade only. The leaves can burn in bright sunlight.
- Blooms April to May. Can be invasive.
- Height 6 to 18 inches.
- Propagates easily from seed.

LAMIUM, DEAD NETTLE, SPOTTED NETTLE
(Lamium maculatum)

This member of the mint family is native in Europe and Asia. The name dead nettle comes from the fact that the leaves don't sting the skin when touched like other nettles tend to do. Named varieties of *L. maculatum* such as 'White Nancy,' 'Beacon Silver' and 'Pink Pewter' are less invasive. Lamium is nice as a ground cover or in a hanging basket, and can be evergreen in mild winter areas.

Yellow archangel (*Lamium galeobdolon*) is another creeping ground cover with silver striped, heart-shaped leaves. Small hooded yellow flowers bloom in April. It too, grows well in sun or shade in rich or poor soil with good drainage.

- Foliage is long, heart-shaped at the bases with green margins surrounding silver or green leaves with a mottled appearance. Pink or white blooms appear whorled on spikes.
- Thrives in dry shade in rich or poor soil with good drainage.
- Blooms late May to late July.
- Grows to 6 to 8 inches high.
- Propagate by division. Spreads easily via creeping roots.

$\mathcal{L}$UPINE
(Lupinus 'Russell Hybrids')

Originally developed by the English breeder, George Russell. Russell lupines are the perennial relatives of the Texas bluebonnet (*Lupinus texensis*) and *Lupinus polyphyllus* which is naturalized from California to British Columbia.

Lupines will tolerate a dry, alkaline soil but prefer a neutral to slightly acidic soil. May be shorter lived in hot-summer climates, so give the plants a light mulch. Allow some space between plants to provide air circulation and avoid possible mildew problems.

Self-sown seedlings will usually revert to their original blue or white colors. Lupine seed coats are hard. To assist germination, soak the seeds in warm water or scratch the seed coat with a file before planting.

- Flowers blue, pink, red, white, yellow, and bi-colors. Dark green foliage is bushy at the base.
- Requires well-drained soil in a cool location with sun or afternoon shade.
- Blooms May to June.
- Height 18 inches to 3 feet.
- Under ideal conditions, Russell lupines will self-sow readily.

 **Attracts hummingbirds and butterflies.**

Resists deer.

Lupine seeds and seed pods are poisonous. L. leucophyllus (velvet or woolly-leafed lupine)–the most toxic of the Lupine genus– is poisonous during all stages of growth.

MONTBRETIA
(Crocosmia crocosmiiflora)

Native to open grasslands in South Africa. Appreciates a winter mulch in colder climates. Flowers are long-lasting and make excellent cut flowers.

- Vigorous, brightly colored red or dark yellow flowers on strong, wiry stems, among long, sword-like foliage.
- Prefers moist, well-drained soil in full sun.
- Blooms April to July, depending on variety.
- Height 2 to 3 feet.
- Propagate by dividing plants in the spring just before growth starts.

Attracts hummingbirds. *Resists deer.*

ORIENTAL POPPY
(Papaver orientale)

Native to Southwest Asia. Poor drainage, especially in the winter, can kill the plants. Take care to water plants at the roots. Water left on the leaves invites bacterial infection. Find a permanent place for Oriental poppies. Their long taproots don't like to be disturbed.

Foliage dies back in the heat of summer. Can rejuvenate in early fall and even bloom again if soil is fertile.

Poppies exude a milky sap when cut. Singe the end of the cut flower stalk with the flame of a candle or a match to seal and then arrange the flower in a vase. If you need to shorten the stem, singe the stem with the small flame again.

The seed pods make an interesting addition to dried flower arrangements.

- Flowers large, crepe paper-type, in colors of apricot, salmon, pink, red, white, or orange. Foliage can be light green to grayish green and hairy.
- Plant the crowns in full sun about 3 inches deep in average soil that has excellent drainage.
- Blooms May to June.
- Height 2 to 3 feet.
- Propagate by division in late fall.

Resists deer and rabbits.

$\mathcal{P}$EONY
(Paeonia hybrids)

Peonies have a long history. There are some cultivars of the European species (*Paeonia mascula* and *P. officinalis*) that have been grown for centuries. However, most of the species that have been cultivated for the past 150 years are derivatives of the Chinese peony, *P. lactiflora* (also called *P. albiflora*) which were introduced to Europe between 1750 and 1850. In the early 1800's, British and Continental European gardeners collected all of the peonies they could find and began hybridizing them. By 1850, many cultivars were available.

Blooms come in five basic flower forms: doubles, semi-doubles, Japanese, anemone or single.

Fertilize with bone meal in spring prior to flowering and in early fall.

A late frost with a rapidly warming morning sun can result in the loss of flower buds. To prevent this, plant peonies in a spot that shelters them from the morning sun or cover them with wet newspapers to slow down the thawing process.

Don't expect flowers the first year after planting, but be patient. They'll give a beautiful show during the second or third season and for decades thereafter.

Since the flowers are so long-lived, prepare the soil at least 18 inches deep. Then plant the tuber with the eyes no more than 2 inches deep. The plants will fail to bloom if planted any deeper.

Peonies provide a three season interest. Emerging foliage has a lovely red tinge. During bloom, foliage is dark green and lush. Finally during the fall, the leaves turn to a red to reddish bronze.

Some heavier flowered cultivars require staking. Most peonies are sweetly fragrant. Cut the plants to the ground in the fall to prevent botrytis infection. Check the water level in a vase full of cut peonies every day. The cut flowers take up a lot of water. Pastel colored flowers fare better in light shade as the colors may fade in full sun. These extremely long-lived plants are known to live a century or more.

- Flowers red, pink, or white with new shades of yellow.
- Grows in full sun or light shade in rich, well-drained, loamy soil.
- Blooms June to July.
- Height 2 to 4 feet.
- Propagate by division in early fall.

Flower buds have a sweet sap that attracts ants. The ants eat the sap, helping the peony bud to open into full flower.

PLANTAIN LILY
(Hosta spp.)

This member of the lily family is native to Japan. Hostas can be used as an edging, low hedge, ground cover, border accent or among trees.

Blue and variegated foliage cultivars grow best in full shade. Some cultivars are tolerant of some sun, but all hostas like extra water during dry, hot summers. Hostas do best in well-drained, rich, moist soil. Crown rot can occur if soil is too soggy.

Find a permanent place for hostas. Propagate 1 to 3 year old plants. Older plants have tough crowns that are difficult to separate. In the proper environment, Hostas can live for 30 years or more.

Long-lasting flowers are about 1-1/2 inches long on short, straight stems. *H. plantaginea* has fragrant flowers.

Most cultivars grow from 1 to 2 feet, but there are some that are as short as 3 to 4 inches and some that grow up to five feet tall.

Planted with spring flowering bulbs, hosta leaves unfurl about the same time bulb leaves start to yellow.

- Flowers blue, green, lavender or white.
- Grows in full to light shade, prefers acid soil, good for north side of house.
- Blooms June to August.
- Height 1 to 2 feet.
- Propagate by division.

🐰 *Rabbit resistant.*

PRIMROSE
(Primula polyantha)

The genus *Primula* contains several hundred species ranging in height from 3 inches to 3 feet that are native to Europe. Also commonly called English primrose. Primroses need shelter from the winds as they can break flower stalks. Looks best when planted en masse in the field. Grows well in containers. Can be evergreen if the temperatures do not fall below 15°F. The Barnhaven strain tends to be longer lived than the Pacific Giant strain. Seeds germinate best when exposed to light.

- Flowers apricot, purple, pink, lavender or white. Foliage is bright green and forms rosettes around the base of the plant.
- Prefers cool, moist, acidic, rich soils with good drainage. Requires afternoon shade.
- Blooms April to May.
- Height 4 to 8 inches.
- Propagate by taking root cuttings, division.

ROCKCRESS
(Arabis caucasica)

Native from the Mediterranean region to Iran. Good ground cover choice for rock gardens, especially when planted in front of daffodils and other spring flowering bulbs. Can also be grown on rock walls.

Shear plants by one half after flowering to promote new growth and bushiness. Can be evergreen. Grow in any well-drained soil in full sun. Will tolerate hot, dry conditions and infertile soils. Fertilize monthly.

- Pink, white or rose colored flowers with gray foliage.
- Full sun, tolerates dry conditions.
- Blooms April to May.
- Height 6 inches.
- Propagate by division.

ROCKCRESS, FALSE
(Aubrieta deltoidea)

Dividing false rockcress can be done but it is difficult. Try taking cuttings in summer or sow seeds in the late spring. 'Novalis Blue' is a variety that grows well from seed.

Plant false rockcress in well-drained soil with average fertility. They actually prefer neutral to slightly alkaline soils. Mulch during dry times to keep the root zone cool.

Shear off flowers by one half before they set seed. After shearing, topdress with a mixture of sandy soil and bone meal.

- Rose, lavender long-blooming flowers over evergreen, gray-green foliage.
- Plant in full sun. Tolerates some dryness after bloom but water well before and during bloom.
- Blooms April to May.
- Height 2 to 6 inches.
- Propagate by taking cuttings or from seed.

Sea Pink
(Armeria maritima)

Native to the seacoasts of Europe, Asia Minor and Northern Africa. This member of the leadwort family can also be called common thrift.

Spreads by short runners into clumps about 1 foot across. The center of the plant dies out in 3 to 4 years. Give sea pink moderate amounts of water. In moist soils, the center of the plant will tend to die out faster, necessitating division.

This relatively care-free plant does require perfect drainage—it may rot in a soggy soil. Requires no fertilizer. Keep deadheaded for continual blooming. Excellent for edging. Can withstand windier areas of the garden. If starting from seed, soak the seeds in warm water for a few hours before planting.

- Hardy, evergreen plant that forms dense cushions of grasslike foliage. Small white, pink or rose colored rounded flowers about 1 inch in diameter on short stems.
- Prefers sandy soil. Best in dry, infertile soil and full sun.
- Flowers prolifically in May and June.
- Height 4 inches to 2 feet.
- Propagate by division or by seed.

Attracts butterflies.   **Deer resistant.**

Silver Mound
(Artemisia schmidtiana)

This member of the daisy family is native to Japan. It can also be called angel's hair or wormwood. The foliage makes an interesting addition to dried flower arrangements or as a filler for wreaths. *A. schmidtiana* foliage is finer cut than 'Silver King' (*A. ludoviciana*) and is not invasive.

'Powis Castle' is a hybrid of *A. absinthium* and *A. arborescens*. It doesn't creep into areas where it is not wanted and has aromatic foliage. It grows to 2 to 3 feet tall and makes a beautiful backdrop for brightly colored flowers.

Pinching plants in late spring to early summer will encourage bushiness. Use the pinchings to propagate new plants.

Must have excellent drainage or the roots and foliage may rot. This is especially true in the winter.

- Beautiful, fragrant, silvery-gray foliage in dense mounds. Leaves have a very soft, feathery texture.
- Prefers sandy, non-fertile soil.
- Inconspicuous flowers in late May to early June.
- Height 10 to 12 inches.
- Propagate with stem cuttings.

SPIDERWORT
(Tradescantia virginiana)

Spiderwort is native to the eastern United States and can also be known as *T. andersoniana*. The long, arching leaves resemble spider legs, hence the name spiderwort.

Bloom clusters are about 1 inch wide, and each flower lasts only a day. However the plant produces many flower buds, so blooming usually lasts all summer long. Rampant spread is best avoided by planting in drier, less fertile soil. After blooming, cut the plants down to about 6 inches. This promotes a more compact habit and may encourage more blooms.

- Flowers blue, pink, purple, white, lavender, or red. Leaves are dark green and straplike.
- Requires moist soil and grows best in shady areas.
- Blooms May to July.
- Height 18 inches to 3 feet. Spreads becoming very full.
- Propagate by dividing established plants.

SUNROSE
(Helianthemum nummularium)

Evergreen or semi-evergreen native to alpine meadows in North and South America, Europe, Asia and North Africa. Can also be sold under the name rockrose.

Each blossom only lasts one day, but new buds will continue to open. Shear back plants after flowering to encourage a fall blooming.

Good plant for rock gardens, rock walls, as a ground cover or in containers.

Plant in well-drained, neutral to alkaline soil of average fertility in full sun. Give sunroses a winter mulch.

- Flowers apricot, orange, pink, red, white and yellow.
- Tolerates heat and dry soil.
- Blooms May to July.
- Height 6 to 8 inches.
- Propagate by rooting cuttings or by seed.

SWEET VIOLET
(Viola odorata)

The genus, *Viola* contains over 500 species that are native to various habitats worldwide. *V. odorata* may be native to Western and Southern Europe. Plants spread by runners that root at the joints. Remove runners and spent flowers for a nice bloom the next spring. For heavier bloom, feed in the very early spring with a complete fertilizer.

- Flowers violet, purple, pink, rose and white over heart-shaped, dark green leaves.
- Grow in shade with moist or dry soil.
- Blooms April to May.
- Height 6 to 10 inches.
- Propagate by division.

WALLFLOWER
(Erysimum 'Bowles' Mauve')

Wallflowers are members of the mustard family. The genus name, *Erysimum* now contains about 80 species including the members of the *Cheiranthus* genus and are native to Europe and Asia.

Blooms from base of stem up through tip, sometimes blooming itself to death. Plant becomes quite leggy if not sheared at least once during blooming season.

Somewhat drought tolerant, wallflowers are ideal for rock gardens. These plants also make a good choice for windier areas of the garden.

The name "Erysimum" comes from the Greek word "eryomai" meaning help or save. Early European physicians thought certain species of *Erysimum* had medicinal properties.

- Mauve-pink, narrow flower clusters on erect stems over grayish-green, finely toothed, hairy leaves.
- Prefers well-drained limy soil in full sun to part shade.
- Blooms May to September.
- Height to 3 feet.
- Propagate by seed or division.

🦌 *Deer resistant.*

ANISE HYSSOP
(Agastache foeniculum)

Native to hilly, drier regions of North America. The botanical name refers to fennel (*Foeniculum vulgare*) which anise hyssop resembles in its scent. Try steeping the leaves in an herbal tea. In colder areas, mulch plants for winter protection.

- Flower spikes have dense clusters of lilac-blue or white flowers over coarsely toothed leaves.
- Plant in full sun to part shade in a rich, moist, well-drained soil.
- Blooms in July.
- Height 2 1/2 to 3 feet tall.
- Propagate by planting root cuttings or allowing the plants to self-sow.

 Attracts butterflies, hummingbirds and bees.

BLACK-EYED SUSANS
(Rudbeckia fulgida)

Found in light woodlands and moist meadows in North America. Keep spent flowers removed for continuous blooming. Flowers are suitable for drying, or try them in fresh arrangements.

Can tolerate various soil conditions but grow best in rich, well-drained soil in full sun. Even tolerates mildly salty soils.

Useful in the back of the border, naturalizing in a wildflower meadow, as a screen or hedge.

- Flowers yellow, maroon or bi-color.
- Grows in sun or light shade.
- Blooms July to September.
- Height 2-1/2 to 4 feet.
- Propagate by division or seed.

Attracts hummingbirds.

BLANKET FLOWER
(Gaillardia grandiflora)

Native to mountainous West and the Southeastern United States. Remove faded blooms for continuous flowering throughout summer, or try allowing the flowers to go to seed. Seed heads add nice winter interest to the garden. Does not perform well in soggy soil. Divide every 2 to 3 years to maintain longevity.

- Colorful yellow, red and maroon flowers.
- Vigorous plant for poor, well-drained soils. Adapts well to drought and heat.
- Blooms June to frost.
- Height 2 to 3 feet.
- Propagate by seed or division.

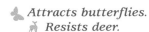 **Attracts butterflies.**
Resists deer.

BLUE STAR CREEPER
(Isotoma fluviatilis or Laurentia fluviatilis)

Recently re-named *Pratia pedunculata*. Most species of *Pratia* were introduced from moist, shady places in Africa, Asia, New Zealand and South America. Blue star creeper can take light foot traffic which makes it perfect for planting between paving stones. Will provide full ground coverage if planted 6 to 12 inches apart. Fertilize monthly.

- Tiny blue flowers on a beautiful dense carpet of small green foliage.
- Sun or partial shade. Prefers moist conditions.
- Blooms from May to September.
- Height 3 inches.
- Propagate by division.

CARDINAL FLOWER
(Lobelia cardinalis)

Native to bogs in Eastern United States. This relatively short-lived flower will self-sow only in optimum conditions. Naturalizes well in boggy wildflower meadows and along stream banks.

- Red flowers over leaves that have dark green to reddish-bronze hues.
- Requires constant moisture and rich soil. Grows best with afternoon shade.
- Blooms from July to early fall.
- Height 3 to 4 feet.
- Propagate by division or by bud cuttings.

 **Attracts hummingbirds.**

Cardinal flowers may contain poisonous alkaloids.

CATMINT
(Nepeta faassenii or N. mussinii)

Nepeta is a large genus of the mint family which contains approximately 250 species native to almost all types of habitats in the Northern Hemisphere.

Silvery, gray-green foliage can be hairy, and is pleasantly aromatic. Flowers are scented as well. Catmint is not as attractive to cats as catnip (*N. cataria*) but sometimes you'll see a feline roll around in its leaves. New plantings may need protection from cats the first year so they can get established.

To encourage successive blooms, cut flower stalks all the way down to the foliage after blooming. Performs well in rock gardens, for edging and as a ground cover. To contain its vigorous nature, plant in drier soils. Catmint appreciates a light winter mulch and can tolerate salty soils.

- Bloom spikes of pale, lavender-blue flowers with darker purple spots.
- Grows in any type soil as long as it's well-drained and has full sun or part shade.
- Blooms June to late August.
- Height 12 to 18 inches.
- Propagate by division in spring or summer.

CONEFLOWER, PURPLE
(Echinacea purpurea)

Native from Iowa to Ohio, south to Louisiana and Georgia. Seed heads look nice dried. Can also be left on the plant to create winter interest and food for goldfinches. Tolerates wind-prone areas of the garden.

- Flowers purple, crimson, or white.
- Tolerates dry soils and heat. Plant in full sun.
- Blooms July to September.
- Height 2 to 3 feet.
- Propagate by division.

 Attracts bees and butterflies.
Resists deer.

COREOPSIS OR TICKSEED
(Coreopsis lanceolata)

Genus of about 100 species of the *Asteraceae* family. Native from Michigan south to Florida and New Mexico. Continuous bloomer, especially when dead-headed.

C. lanceolata doesn't bloom as well if the soil is too rich. When established, coreopsis tolerates poor, dry soil. Grows best in full sun and heat.

Yellow with single, daisy-like flowers (*C. lanceolata*) or double flowers (*C. grandiflora*).

- Yellow flowers on medium-green upright stems.
- Plant in well-drained soils. Prefers sun and adapts to drought conditions.
- Blooms June to September.
- Height 2 to 3 feet.
- Propagate by seed, division or root cuttings.

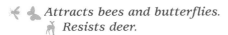 ***Attracts bees and butterflies.***
Resists deer.

CREEPING THYME
(Thymus serpyllum)

Creeping thyme can tolerate light foot traffic and, emits a nice fragrance when crushed. It also grows well when planted in a rock garden or on a rock wall. Can also be known as mother of thyme.

- Pink or purple flowers.
- Tolerates poor, dry soils in full sun.
- Blooms May to June.
- Height 2 to 6 inches.
- Propagate by division or seeds.

Attracts bees.

FEVERFEW
(Tanacetum parthenium)
Used to prevent and treat migraine headaches, fevers.

ANISE HYSSOP
(Agastache foeniculum)
A delicious herb tea; attracts bees; used for licorice flavoring. Used medicinally to energize and cool the body and for respiratory problems.

BERGAMOT
(Monarda didyma)
Blossoms are edible, excellent flavoring for beans and salads. Used as a tea to improve digestion, and to ease colds.

BLOODROOT
(Cimicifuga racemosa)
Used as a bitter tonic for aches and pains, coughing, and fevers.

COLUMBINE
(Aquilegia spp.)
Colorful flowers used for potpourris

DELPHINIUM AND LARKSPUR
(Delphinium spp.)
A prominent in the herb garden for colorful potpourris.

FOXGLOVE
(Digitalis purpurea)
As a medicinal, provides digitalis.

INDIGO, WILD
(Baptisia tinctoria)
Leaves, pod and bark are highly valued for dye.

LAMB'S EAR
(Stachys spp.)
Gray, fuzzy foliage valued for potpourri.

LAVENDER COTTON
(Santolina spp.)
Excellent gray color used by herbalists.

SWEET VIOLET
(Viola odorota)
Deliciously sweet scent is important to connoisseurs of herbal fragrances.

GOLDENROD
(Solidago odora)
Flowers used for tea.

EVENING PRIMROSE
(Oenothera biennis)
Taproot and young leaves are edible. The seed oil is used to treat PMS, hyperactivity, atopic eczema, acne and rheumatoid arthritis.

LADYS MANTLE
(Alchemilla xanthochlora)
Used as an astringent to stop bleeding, menstrual pain and irregularities. Drops of dew in the leaves were known as an "alchemist's elixir" (thus the Latin genus name)

LAVENDER
(Lavandula spp.)
Used to calm the nerves and for headaches, soothes burns, cuts and induces sleep. Highly valued by herbalists for scent and color.

PURPLE CONEFLOWER
(Echinacea spp.)
One of the most important of American medicinal plants. Both the roots and aerial parts are used medicinally. Used by Plains, Kiawa and Sioux Indians as an antidote for snake bites, stings, toothaches, sore throat, colds, cancers and more. All *echinaceas* are used as general blood purifiers for support and stimulation of the immune system and to treat the common cold.

ST. JOHNS WORT
(Hypericum perforatum)
Used since ancient times for its antidepressant properties; healing wounds and as an antiviral. It penetrates to nerve endings and is used as an antispasmodic and antidepressant sedative.

WORMWOOD
(Artemisia absinthium)
A Biblical bitter herb was used to flavor absinthe liqueur. Southernwood (A. Abrotanum) is lemon-scented and used in potpourris.

YARROW
(Achillea millefolium) (white version is "Proa")
Known as the "fever herb," white-flowered varieties are preferred by herbalists. Used for colds, fevers and to heal wounds. Topically applied, crushed flower tops and leaves stop bleeding.

A family is a place where minds come in contact with one another. If these minds love one another the home will be as beautiful as a flower garden. But if these minds get out of harmony with one another it is like a storm that plays havoc with the garden.

Buddha

DAYLILY
(Hemerocallis spp.)

Found naturally in marsh river valleys, forest margins, mountainous areas and meadow lands in China, Korea and Japan.

The first recorded hybridization of daylilies was made by an English schoolteacher named George Yeld. Two years later, he introduced 'Apricot,' the first cultivar. Over 30,000 cultivars are now available.

The latest daylily cultivars are called tetraploids or tetras. They have twice the amount of chromosomes which result in larger, heavier textured flowers as well as more blooms per stem.

Many of the numerous cultivars are evergreen or semi-evergreen. Most in this zone are herbaceous. Daylilies are extremely adaptable, low maintenance plants. They are excellent for naturalizing or massed for an accent. Some cultivars are salt tolerant.

Flowers generally last one day, many varieties flower repeatedly throughout season. Flowers are single or double and come in a wide range of colors: yellow, orange, peach, white, light green, clear pink, purple and red.

Cut stems with well developed flower buds for fresh arrangements. Flowers will open on successive days, though each flower will be slightly smaller than the preceding one.

Daylilies have a clump-forming or rhizomatous habit which makes them easy to increase by division. These plants can be divided almost anytime except during the heat of the summer.

- Lily-like flowers in wide range of colors on arching, strap-like, medium green leaves.
- Tolerates dry soil, will grow in full sun or light shade.
- Blooms June to August.
- Height 2 to 4 feet.
- Propagate by division.

Resists rabbits and deer.

FLAX
(Linum spp.)

Genus of about 200 species. *L. usitatissimum* is the plant used to extract linseed oil.

- Yellow or light-blue flowers on clump-forming plants with feathery foliage.
- Tolerates heat and dry soil, native to the Great Basin, flowers last one day.
- Blooms May to September.
- Height 2 to 2-1/2 feet.
- Very dependable, short-lived but rampant self-seeder.

FOXGLOVE
(Digitalis purpurea)

This member of the snapdragon family makes a good plant for the back of the garden.

Native to Western Mediterranean region, Europe, West Africa and Central Asia. Foxgloves self-sow easily and are technically biennial.

Deadhead spent blooms for second round of smaller blooms. Foxgloves may require staking in wind-prone areas.

Foxgloves may have gotten their name from an old northern legend. It claims that bad fairies gave foxglove blossoms to the fox to put on his toes, so he might soften his tread while he hunted for prey.

- Tall spikes of lavender, pink, purple, or white tubular flowers.
- Prefers slightly acid, well-drained soil with afternoon shade.
- Blooms June to July.
- Height 2 to 4 feet.
- Propagate by seed.

  Attracts hummingbirds.
  Resists rabbits and deer.

All parts of foxglove are poisonous. First year growth has been mistaken for comfrey (Symphitum officinale) with fatal results. Ingestion of this plant can be fatal at any growth stage, but foxglove is most toxic just before the seeds ripen. The upper leaves of the stem are also more toxic than the lower leaves. Contact with the skin may cause irritation to sensitive individuals.

Gay Feather
(Liatris spicata)

Native to Eastern North American meadows and marsh edges, this member of the daisy family makes a good spiky addition to the garden. It is also commonly called blazing star.

If starting plants from seed, the seeds must be chilled for several weeks in the refrigerator. Flower spikes open from the top down.

- Flowers are tall with white or reddish-purple plumes over ribbon-like foliage.
- Tolerates heat and poor, dry soil. Plant in full sun or light shade. Does not tolerate wet conditions.
- Blooms July to August.
- Height 1 to 5 feet, depending on variety.
- Propagate by division in early spring or by seed.

 Attracts butterflies and bees.

When cutting a bloom for bouquets, leave two-thirds of the stem behind to help the plant produce food for itself.

Geum
(Geum coccineum)

This species is native to the mountains of Chile while *G. triflorum* is native to the Rocky Mountain region of North America. Geum flowers profusely. Fertilize monthly and remove spent flowers constantly for continuous bloom. Can be evergreen except in areas with the coldest winters. Likes extra water in hot, dry conditions.

Newer hybrids can go many years without division which is best done in late summer.

- Orange, red or yellow flowers on bright green foliage.
- Prefers soils rich in organic matter.
- Blooms May to July.
- Height 1 to 2 feet.
- Propagates rapidly by seed.

Sometimes Cranesbill geranium *is confused with* Pelargonium geranium. *Pelargoniums have showier flowers with two petals pointing in one direction while three point in the opposite direction.* Cranesbills *have five overlapping petals that look alike.* Pelargoniums *are not hardy and are grown as annuals.*

Geranium
(Cranesbill spp.)

This European and Asian native is very hardy and requires minimal care. The shape of the flower stem gives this plant its name—the stem is in the shape of a crane's bill. Cut back to about one-half height after flowering. *G. macrorrhizum, G. sanguineum* and *G. endressi* are drought tolerant.

- Pink, magenta, lilac or blue flowers over outstanding foliage of deep-cut leaves that turn red in fall (dependent on cultivar).
- Prefers moist soil and full sun with afternoon shade.
- Blooms May to August.
- Height 8 to 24 inches, dependent on cultivar.
- Propagate by division or stem cuttings in spring or fall.

Resists deer.

Globe Thistle
(Echinops exaltus)

This Russian native is excellent for dried arrangements. Cutting the flowers all the way to the base—just before they are fully open—will encourage a second blooming.

These plants are excellent as a garden accent. Give them support in the windier areas of the garden. Established plants will tolerate dry periods due to their very strong roots that can grow to one foot deep.

- Globular, dark-blue flower heads.
- Prefers well-drained, average soil in full sun.
- Blooms July to September.
- Height 2 to 4 feet.
- Propagate by root cuttings or division in spring.

Attracts butterflies.

GLORIOSA DAISY
(Rudbeckia hirta)

Descendants of wild plants from the Eastern United States, gloriosa daisies are excellent for naturalizing. Can be drought tolerant. These plants are very similar to black-eyed Susans. Turn to page 48 for additional notes.

- Clear yellow flowers with deep brown centers.
- Does well in all types of soil, sun or shade.
- Blooms June to frost.
- Height 2 to 3 feet.
- Propagate by seed or division.

HELIOPSIS, OXEYE
(Heliopsis helianthoides)

Heliopsis is native to dry prairies and open woodlands in Eastern North America. This plant provides long lasting cut flowers.

- Yellow or orange flowers with brown centers.
- Grows in full sun, intolerant of dry, infertile soil. Needs protection in winter.
- Blooms July to frost.
- Height 3 to 4 feet.
- Propagate by division.

*H*ERON'S BILL
(Erodium spp.)

Native to the Balearic Islands and Corsica. Heron's bill can also be found in mountainous regions of Europe and Central Asia. This dainty plant forms a creeping mat that works well in the rock garden.

- Tiny pink flowers on delicate silvery foliage.
- Adapts well to sun and dry soils.
- Blooms May to June.
- Height 3 inches.
- Propagate by division.

*H*OLLYHOCK
(Alcea rosea)

This genus contains about 30 species and is native to China. For a second blooming in September, cut the flower stalk just above the ground in July. Continue to feed and water the plants. Two bloomings are demanding upon the plants, so make sure they have the best possible conditions. The flower stalks require staking in wind-prone areas. Seeds germinate best when exposed to light. Somewhat similar to *Malvaceae alcea* or hollyhock mallow.

- Single or double flowers come in red, pink, purple, white or yellow.
- Tolerates dry soil conditions, but prefers regular water and grows best in full sun.
- Blooms July to September.
- Height 3 to 9 feet.
- Short-lived perennial or biennial; reseeds easily.

 Attracts butterflies, bees and hummingbirds.

*J*ACOB'S *L*ADDER
(Polemonium caeruleum)

Native to Central and Northern Europe and the western region of North America.

- Blue or white flowers.
- Grows in shade and prefers cool, moist soils. Requires good drainage.
- Blooms in June.
- Height 1-1/2 to 2-1/2 feet.
- Propagate by division.

*J*APANESE *I*RIS
(Iris kaempferi)

Japanese irises demand more moisture than bearded irises and will grow in water gardens. Flowers will grow 6 feet tall, given ideal conditions.

- Showy flowers without beards. Flowers are single, double or peony-style in white, pink, purple and blue.
- Prefers moist, slightly boggy conditions and acidic soil in partial shade.
- Blooms June to August.
- Height 24 to 36 inches tall.
- Propagate by division of rhizomes.

Japanese iris require acidic or neutral soil AND water. If soil or water is alkaline, apply aluminum sulfate or iron sulfate (1 oz. to 2 gal. of water) several times during growing season.

Jupiter's Beard
(Centranthus ruber)

From dry, sunny slopes in Southern Europe, the Mediterranean, Northwest Africa and Southwest Asia, this plant can be listed as red valerian (*Valeriana coccinea*) or keys of heaven.

Centranthus has a bushy, upright habit. It is good for tough spots but is invasive. It thrives in infertile, alkaline soils and self sows rampantly with small, dandelion-like seeds.

- Deep crimson, pink or white flowers.
- Plant in full sun.
- Blooms June to July.
- Height to 3 feet.
- Propagate by division.

 Attracts butterflies and bees.
Resists deer.

Knautia
(Knautia macedonica)

This native to Romania and the Balkans is a member of the *Dipsacaceae* family. Knautia is very similar to the pincushion flower in appearance.

Another member of this genus, *K. arvensis*, or field scabious, has violet-blue flowers and is considered a nuisance weed in some regions.

- Rich, dark purple-red flower heads on delicate stems over dark green foliage. Leaf tips turn bronze in fall.
- Prefers full sun with well-drained, fertile soil.
- Blooms July through frost.
- Height 2 to 4 feet.
- Propagate by division every three to four years.

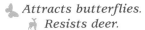 *Attracts butterflies.*
Resists deer.

*L*AMB'S *E*ARS, *W*OOLLY *B*ETONY
(Stachys byzantina, S. lanata, S. olympica)

Native to Turkey and Southwestern Asia, lamb's ears do well in rock gardens or for edging. Try them with darker green leafed plants or different leaf-shaped plants for contrast.

Variety 'Silver Carpet' does not produce flowers. 'Helen Von Stein' is a vigorous cultivar with broad foliage. It seldom blooms and is rot resistant. *Stachys grandiflora* (big betony) is taller than *S. byzantina* and has showier flowers.

- Velvety, spreading foliage resembling lamb's ears with tall spikes of vivid pink or purple flowers.
- Prefers dry soils in sun to part shade. Moist soils cause centers to rot.
- Cultivated for foliage rather than bloom.
- Forms mat 12 to 15 inches tall.
- Propagates rapidly by seed or division.

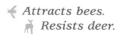 *Attracts bees.*
Resists deer.

*L*AVENDER
(Lavandula spp.)

Try this native to Southern Europe as a border plant, as a low growing hedge or in a rock garden. The latest lavender group includes *Lavendula X intermedia* which is commonly called "lavandins." Lavandins have a superior fragrance, are hardy to 0°F and have longer flower spikes.

Flowers are perfect for fresh or dried arrangements. Dry lavender flowers on a flat screen or on several layers of absorbent paper.

Cut back stems by one-third in early spring to rejuvenate plant.

Wrap some freshly harvested lavender flowers in a muslin bag or three thickness of cheesecloth and steep in a warm bath.

- Flowers lavender or purple.
- Grows in well-drained soils and full sun.
- Blooms June to frost.
- Height 1 to 3 feet.
- Propagate using softwood cuttings.

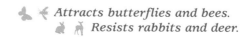 *Attracts butterflies and bees.*
Resists rabbits and deer.

Lavandula angustifolia (L. officinalis, L. spica, L. vera) or English lavender is the most widely planted for the fragrance of sachets and perfumes.

***

Lavender Rose potpourri
4 c. Lavender flowers
2 c. Rose petals
2 c. Rosemary
1 oz. Orris Root

Herbal Potpourri
2 c. Thyme
1 c. Rosemary
1/2 c. Lavender
1 c. Mint
1/4 c. Tansy
1/4 c. Whole cloves
1/2 oz. Orris Root

ℒAVENDER 𝒞OTTON
(Santolina chamaecyparissus)

Prune to maintain shape after flowering. Also can be listed as *S. incana*.

S. rosmarinifolius or *S. virens* has narrower, deep green leaves and looks like a puff of green smoke.

Foliage adds a musky scent to sachets.

- Compact, spreading plants with aromatic, stiff, gray-green foliage with small, yellow, button-like flowers.
- Prefers dry, stony soils with excellent drainage and room for air circulation.
- Blooms June to August.
- Can grow from 1-1/2 to 2 feet, but looks its best kept at 1 foot high.
- Propagate from cuttings.

𝓜ALLOW
(Malva spp.)

Native mostly to Southern Europe. Mallow is related to and resembles Hollyhock, but has a bushier habit.

Malva alcea 'Fastigiata' has been grown in gardens since 1820. *Malva moschata* 'Alba', a bushy plant with clear white flowers, dates back to the 1600's.

- Purple, blue, pink or white flowers.
- Takes full sun to part shade. Requires excellent drainage in average soil with moderate water.
- Blooms June to September.
- Grows 3 to 4 feet.
- Propagate from seed.

MALTESE CROSS
(Lychnis chalcedonica)

Native to Northern Russia. Consistent removal of spent flowers will encourage a second blooming in August. Foliage provides continual interest for three seasons.

- Red or white flowers form dense, brilliantly colored clusters on compact plants.
- Grows best in moist, well-drained soil with full sun or part shade.
- Blooms June to July.
- Height 2 to 3 feet.
- Readily self-seeds, can become invasive.

MAT DAISY
(Anacyclus depressus)

Anacyclus is a small genus containing 9 species, native to mountainous regions of the Mediterranean. Can be commonly known as Mount Atlas daisy or just Atlas daisy. Scientifically, mat daisies can be known as *Anacyclus pyrethrum*.

Mat daisies require perfect drainage, especially in winter. They will rot in cold, soggy soils. They require little water—if at all—once established.

Excellent for borders, rock gardens, edging or try mat daisies as a ground cover. White petals on the front are red with a white stripe on the back.

Many parts of the plant contain the chemical pellitorine which herbalists claim increase saliva flow and decrease the pain from toothaches and gum infections.

- White, daisy-like flowers on dense, low-growing, fern-like, gray-green foliage.
- Prefers full sun with a well-drained, somewhat gravelly soil.
- Blooms May to June.
- Height 3 to 4 inches tall.
- Propagate by seed, stem cuttings or by division.

The kiss of the sun for pardon,
The song of the birds for mirth,
One is nearer God's Heart in a garden
Than anywhere else on earth.

Dorothy Frances Gurney
(1858-1932), U.S. Poet.
"God's Garden"

MEADOWSWEET, DROPWORT
(Filipendula vulgaris, F. hexapetala)

This plant is very similar to *Astilbe*. Showy perennial for the border or as an accent plant that tolerates shade. Flower clusters look lovely in fresh or dried arrangements, or leave them on the plant to create a winter interest.

- Feathery clusters of ivory flowers over fern-like foliage.
- Can tolerate drought and poorer soils. Plant in full sun to part shade.
- Blooms May to June.
- Height 18 to 24 inches tall.
- Propagate by division.

When you have a garden, you have a future and when you have a future, you are alive.

Frances Hodgson Burnett

MONKSHOOD
(Aconitum spp.)

Monkshood is one of the oldest garden plants. Some species can be noted as early as 1200. Monkshood needs to be fertilized continuously, especially with phosphorus and potash. Contact with skin may cause irritation.

- Tall spikes of long, bell-shaped, light blue to deep purple flowers on dark green, finely-cut foliage.
- Full sun or filtered light conditions. Intolerant of extreme heat. Prefers moist, well-drained soil.
- Blooms May to September, depending upon variety.
- Height 2 to 4 feet.
- Propagate by division.

All monkshood plant parts are poisonous.

OBEDIENT PLANT, FALSE DRAGONHEAD
(Physostegia virginiana)

Physostegia contains about 12 species which are all native to the Eastern United States. The name *Physostegia* derives from the Greek words "physa" which means bladder and "stege" which means covering. The words describe the calyx which swells and covers the fruit of the plant at maturity. The common name, obedient plant, refers to the flower's habit of remaining in position when twisted on the stem. Obedient plants can be invasive if not kept in check. Divide the clumps every year to keep them contained. These extremely hardy plants make a nice choice for a large border and are lovely in fresh flower arrangements.

- Purple, pink or white flowers on square stems over sharply-toothed, mid-green leaves.
- Grows best in consistently moist, fertile soil with full sun or part shade.
- Blooms July to September.
- Height 3 to 4 feet.
- Propagate by division.

PAINTED DAISY, PYRETHRUM
(Chrysanthemum coccineum)

Member of the daisy family, native to Southwest Asia. Sometimes scientifically called *Tanacetum coccineum*.

- Intense flower colors of crimson, pink, or white. Flowers may be single or double.
- Tolerates dry soil and grows best in full sun. Easy to cultivate.
- Blooms May to June.
- Height 1-1/2 to 2-1/2 feet.
- Propagate by division.

$\mathcal{P}$ENSTEMON, $\mathcal{B}$EARDTONGUE
(Penstemon hartwegii)

Most of the 250 or so species are native to Western United States, Canada and Mexico. Penstemon is a member of the snapdragon family. Remove spent flowers to encourage an autumn bloom and mulch them in the winter to give them some protection.

- Tubular flowers of lavender, pink, purple and red on vertical, slender stalks.
- Grows in sun or light shade, tolerates heat and dry soils.
- Blooms June to July.
- Height 1-1/2 to 3 feet.
- Propagate by seed.

$\curlyvee$ *Attracts hummingbirds.*

$\mathcal{P}$INCUSHION $\mathcal{F}$LOWER
(Scabiosa caucasica)

This member of the teasel family is native to Caucasus. Pincushion flower is one of England's favorite cutting flowers. They can be cut and brought indoors when the flowers are only half open. Removing faded flowers will prolong the plant's bloom. Periodic division will increase the life of the original plant. Pincushion flowers benefit from mulching. *Scabiosa atropurpurea* is a hardy annual strain of *Scabiosa*.

- Flowers light blue, lavender, white and a new light yellow variety. Blooms on slender, airy stems above medium green, dense foliage.
- Grows in sun to part shade and prefers well-drained, fertile soils.
- Blooms June to frost.
- Height 1-1/2 to 2 feet.
- Propagate by division in fall.

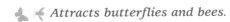 *Attracts butterflies and bees.*

Some species make nice bouquets that can last up to a week in the vase, or try drying Dianthus *flowers. They make a nice base for a spicy potpourri.*

$\mathcal{P}$INK
(Dianthus spp.)

This genus contains more than 200 species native to Asia and Europe.

Smaller species of *Dianthus* are nice additions to rock gardens.

Border type carnations differ from florists' type in that they are bushier and more compact plants.

Most *Dianthus* offer a strong, spicy, clovelike scent. Border carnations, *D. deltoides*, *D. gratianopolitanus*, *D. plumarius*, *D.* 'Rose Bowl', *D.* 'Tiny Rubies' are especially known for fragrance.

Scotch pink or cottage pink *(D. plumarius)* has been cultivated for hundreds of years and has been widely used to develop new hybrids. Native to Central Europe, Scotch pinks bloom from June through October and can grow from 10 to 18 inches tall.

- Flowers rose, purple, pink or white.
- Grows best in rich or organic soils in full sun or light shade with good drainage.
- Blooms June to July.
- Height 12 to 18 inches.
- Propagate by taking cuttings from the tips of growing shoots, by division or from seed.

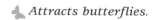 *Attracts butterflies.*

$\mathcal{P}$LUMBAGO
(Cerastostigma plumbaginoides)

Native to Western Asia, can also be commonly called leadwort. Plumbago is very winter hardy, but it doesn't bloom well unless it has a long growing season.

- Blue flowers over green foliage that turns red to bronze in fall.
- Prefers moist, cool growing conditions and light or afternoon shade.
- Blooms July to August.
- Height 6 to 12 inches.
- Propagate by division, just before growth starts.

Plumbago is good groundcover for spring flowering bulbs as it does not bloom until summer.

PRIMROSE, MEXICAN
(Oenothera berlandieri)

Native to dry soils in the Central United States and may rot when conditions are too moist. *O. berlandieri* can also be called *O. speciosa.*

Mexican primrose blooms flowers all summer long. This 6 to 12 inch plant requires minimal care, but can be invasive. After spring blooming, cut the flowers back by one-half height to stimulate new growth. The plant will keep blooming until it feels it has set enough seed pods before senescing.

Its cousin, evening primrose (*O. missouriensis* or *O. macrocarpa*), has broad yellow flowers that open in the evening and close at the end of the next day.

Primroses prefer dry, gravelly soils which make them a perfect addition to the rock garden. They also look nice when cascading over retaining walls.

- Soft pink, cup-shaped flower.
- Tolerates heat, full sun or light shade and dry well-drained soils.
- Blooms May to July.
- Height 6 to 12 inches.
- Propagate by division.

RED HOT POKER
(Kniphofia uvaria)

This South African native can also be called torch lily or poker plant.

- Flowers lemon yellow, creamy white, red and yellow, orange and yellow.
- Grows in full sun, drought tolerant.
- Blooms July to August.
- Height 3 to 4 feet.
- Propagate by division.

Y *Attracts hummingbirds.*
  Resists rabbits.

SAGE
(Salvia spp.)

All *Salvia spp.* can tolerate windy areas of the garden. Looks its best with 6 to 7 plants grouped together. Divide in fall or spring to acquire new plants or to rejuvenate old clumps. The botanical name "Salvia" is rooted in the Latin word "salvare," meaning to heal or to save.

BLUE SAGE
(Salvia azurea grandiflora)

These lovely flowers can be sold under the name of *Salvia pitcheri*. Blue sage flowers dry very well. Hang upside down for best results. Several tip pinches during June and July will improve plant shape and increase number of blooms. Sometimes shows iron deficiencies in alkaline soils. Provide sulfur at planting time if soil is alkaline.

- Blue flowers.
- Grows in full sun, tolerates dry soil when established.
- Blooms July to September.
- Height 2 to 5 feet.
- Propagate by seed or division.

COMMON SAGE
(Salvia officinalis)

Can also be called purple sage. Common sage was used as a meat preservative in ancient times because of its antioxidant properties. Sage was once believed to make life immortal and was so valuable that the Chinese would trade three pounds of their tea for one pound of sage.

The variegated varieties are less cold tolerant and appreciate a winter mulch. They also make an attractive contrast to darker green-leafed plants. 'Aurea' has yellow-green variegated, cream-edged leaves. 'Purpurea' has traditional gray-green leaves with silvery purple leaves scattered within. 'Tricolor' has purple streaks through the white-margined green leaves. Common sage is useful as a culinary herb.

- Lilac-blue flowers bloom on long, silver-green foliage.
- Grows in loose, moist soil of average fertility in full sun to part shade.
- Blooms June to July.
- Height 2 to 3 feet.
- Propagate by seed or division.

Some herbalists suggest that the aromatic leaves of perennial sage soothe muscle stiffness when used in an herbal bath.

The best remedy for those who are afraid, lonely or unhappy is to go outside, somewhere where they can be quiet, alone with the heavens, nature and God. Because only then does one feel that all is as it should be and that God wishes to see people happy, amidst the simple beauty of nature. As long as this exists, and it certanily always will, I know that then there will always be comfort for every sorrow, whatever the circumstances may be. And I firmly believe that nature brings solace in all troubles.

Anne Frank

PERENNIAL SAGE
(Salvia X superba)

This Mediterranean native is also called perennial salvia. Leaves are aromatic when crushed. 'Blue Hills' is nearly everblooming.

- Tiny, densely-whorled flowers on 4 to 8 inch long spikes.
- Grows in loose, moist soil of average fertility in full sun to part shade.
- Blooms July to September.
- Grows 2 to 3 feet tall.
- Propagate by seed or division.

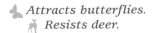 *Attracts butterflies.*
Resists deer.

Shasta Daisy
(Chrysanthemum maximum)

This member of the daisy family is also known scientifically as *C. superbum*. Parents are probably native to Portugal and Pyrenees. There are many different varieties, but double flowering varieties prefer some shade.

Shasta daisy plants will bloom profusely if spent flowers are consistently removed. Cut stems in half to keep plant bushy. Divide when clumps become overcrowded. Germination is best when the seeds are exposed to light.

- White flowers with a gold center.
- Tolerant of dry soil and heat. Prefers full sun and well-drained, loose, fertile soil. Tends to get leggy in light shade.
- Blooms June to August.
- Height 2 to 4 feet.
- Propagate by division.

Shepherd's Crook
(Lysimachia clethroides)

Native to China and Japan, this plant makes an excellent ground cover in moist conditions. It spreads vigorously underground. Plant where containerization is not required. Can also be listed as gooseneck loosestrife.

Purple loosestrife (*Lythrum virgatum*) has become a noxious weed in some regions by choking out native flora. For this reason, the sale of *L. virgatum* is banned in these regions.

- Graceful, curving white racemes on medium green, thick foliage.
- Plant in average, moist, well-drained soil with full sun to part shade.
- Blooms July to August.
- Height 24 to 30 inches.
- Propagate by division.

Sneezeweed does not cause people to sneeze. It blooms around the same time as ragweed–a plant that can induce allergic symptoms like sneezing. However, it can cause severe intestinal discomfort if ingeseted and the leaves may irritate the skin.

SNEEZEWEED
(Helenium autumnale)

Sometimes sold as Helen's flower. Native to marshes and wet meadows of North America.

H. autumnale or common sneezeweed is the most widely cultivated and is specifically native to Canada from British Columbia to Quebec south through the Appalachians to Florida. Bigelow sneezeweed (*H. bigelovii*) is native to the Sierra Nevada mountains from Southern California to Southern Oregon. It is shorter than *H. autumnale* but does have larger flowers.

Sneezeweed flowers are similar to sunflowers with their multi-petaled flowers. The petals have an interesting habit of bending back towards the stem. The flowers are nice for fresh floral arrangements and will provide more blooms if deadheaded regularly.

Species plant seeds will self-sow true, but hybrid seeds will not.

- 1 to 2 inch flowers come in solid red, orange-yellow or bi-colored petals with prominent centers. Leaves are medium to dark green, lance shaped.
- Plant in any moist, fertile soil that is well-drained. Plant in full sun.
- Blooms from late July until frost.
- Height 2 to 5 feet.
- Propagate by division or by seed.

SNOW IN SUMMER
(Cerastium tomentosum)

Snow in summer is native to the Arctic and temperate regions of Europe and North America. It grows just about anywhere in the west and is an excellent choice for rock gardens.

- Bright white, small flowers bloom over mounds of silvery leaves.
- Prefers dry soils in full sun.
- Blooms May to June.
- Height 6 to 8 inches.
- Propagates easily by seed or division.

Summer Blooms

Speedwell
(Veronica spicata)

Genus contains over 250 species mostly native to Europe and Turkey. Speedwell is a fine plant for rock gardens. *Hebe* is a shrub that is commonly called veronica.

- Blue, pink, rose or white flowers.
- Tolerates dry soils, grows in full sun or light shade.
- Blooms June to July.
- Height 10 to 18 inches.
- Propagate by division.

Y **Attracts hummingbirds.**
🦌 **Resists deer.**

Speedwell, Woolly
(Veronica incana)

- Bright blue flowers over silvery leaves.
- Tolerates heat and dry soils, grows best in full sun.
- Blooms June to July.
- Height 6 to 12 inches.
- Propagate by division.

When cutting for fresh arrangements, choose a spike that is only one-third open, and cut during the cooler part of the day.

Summer Phlox
(Phlox paniculata)

Most are native to North America. Flower colors can bleach if exposed to the sun's heat. Lighter colored species can be fragrant.

- Flowers blue, lavender, pink, purple, red or white.
- Grows in full sun, tolerates dry soil.
- Blooms July to August.
- Height 2 to 4 feet.
- Divide clumps when they become overcrowded.

Y 🦋 *Attracts hummingbirds and butterflies.*

SUNFLOWER, MAXIMILLIAN'S
(Helianthus maximilliani)

Native to Central and Southwestern United States. The genus, *Helianthus* contains about 70-80 species and is a member of the Asteraceae family. *Helianthus tuberosum* is commonly called the Jerusalem artichoke, sunchoke or tuberous sunflower. Sunchokes were frequently cultivated by American Indians as a staple for their diet. The Latin name "Helianthus" comes from "helios" which means sun and "anthos" which means flower.

- Blooms are daisy-like with bright yellow petals over mid-green foliage.
- Grow in full sun with a well-drained soil of moderate fertility.
- Blooms July to October.
- Height 8 to 10 feet.
- Divide in spring or take root cuttings to propagate.

SWEETPEA, PERENNIAL
(Lathyrus latifolia)

Good for trellising, fences, or slopes. May escape and become weed.

- Flowers pink, purple, red or white.
- Grows in full sun or light shade and tolerates dry soils.
- Blooms June to September.
- Height vines to 8 feet.
- Propagate with seed.

In poorer soils, dig a trench 12 to 18 inches deep. Mix 1 part peat moss or other soil conditioner to 2 parts native soil. While mixing, add complete commercial fertilizer according to manufacturer's directions. Backfill trench with mix and plant.

$\mathcal{Y}$ARROW
(Achillea spp.)

Yarrow seeds germinate best when exposed to light.

COMMON YARROW
(A. millefolium)

Native to California. The European species has been in cultivation for more than 550 years. Native, dwarf cultivars also available. Forms a growing mat which makes this plant an excellent ground cover.

- Flower color red or white over pleasantly aromatic leaves.
- Tolerant of dry soils and heat. Grows best in full sun.
- Blooms July to August.
- Height 1 to 3 feet.
- Propagate by division.

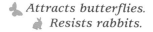 *Attracts butterflies.*
Resists rabbits.

FERNLEAF YARROW
(A. filipendulina)

Native to Asia Minor and Caucasus. May require staking in windy areas.

- Flower color mustard yellow.
- Tolerant of dry soils and heat. Grows best in full sun.
- Blooms July to August.
- Height 4 to 5 feet.
- Propagate by dividing clumps.

WOOLLY YARROW
(A. Tomentosa)

Woolly yarrow makes a nice ground cover that can be mowed. The gray foliage releases a pleasant fragrance when walked upon. Flowers are excellent for fresh or dried arrangements. Tolerates alkaline soils.

- Flower color yellow or golden.
- Tolerant of dry soils and heat. Grows best in full sun.
- Blooms June to July.
- Height 6 to 12 inches.
- Propagate by division.

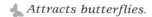 *Attracts butterflies.*

Ornamental Grasses

*O*rnamental grasses have just recently become popular to the perennial garden. And for good reason too! These outstanding perennials are easy to care for, have interesting attributes, and with so many species, there are ornamental grasses available for almost any site.

Ornamental grasses are different from the usual lawn type grasses most gardeners are familiar with. They tend to stay in the same spot and clump like flowering perennials do. These clumps spread slowly over time which allows us to obtain new plants to share with friends or spread to other parts of the garden.

These plants are cultivated for a number of reasons. Some have interesting foliage colors or leaf shapes. Some sprout beautiful seed heads called inflorescence and create autumn interest. Some taller grasses are lovely in the breeze and the gentle rustling sound created when the wind blows is incredibly restful. Whatever the reason, there's always a place to put ornamental grasses in the garden.

Japanese Blood Grass
(Imperata cylindrica 'Rubra')

Excellent in borders or rock gardens, *Imperata* is a genus that contains about 6 species of grasses that are native to the open grasslands of Japan. Can also be known as *Imperata cylindrica* 'Red Baron.' Likes winter mulch, especially when the plants are young.

- Slow growing, rhizomatous plant that grows flat, erect, pointed, bright green blades that have a vivid red margin. Blades turn brown in fall.
- Prefers fertile, moist, well-drained soil in full sun to light shade.
- Flowers are short and silvery, but insignificant.
- Height 12 to 24 inches.
- Propagate by division in spring or early summer.

Japanese Forest Grass
(Hakonechloa macra)

This genus contains only one species which is native to the mountains and forests of Japan. Sometimes this grass is sold under the common name of hakone grass. In fall, they take on a pinkish hue that may persist into winter.

Variegated cultivars produce the best colors in part shade. Prefers acidic soil (pH 5.5-6.0). Likes protection in the winter. Excellent for borders and as an accent plant.

- Soft, graceful, arching, striped yellow and green bladed leaves.
- Prefers fertile, moist, well-drained soil in sun or light shade.
- Blooms August to September, but not remarkable.
- Height to 18 inches.
- Propagate by division.

Maiden Grass, Morning Light Grass, Silver Grass
(Miscanthaus sinensis)

Native to both China and Japan. The fine, complex pattern of this plants' blades fills the negative spaces among the perennials and knits the garden together.

Most species of *Miscanthus* reach full size by August. After blooming, the plants begin to go dormant and turn a wheat color. The flowers are useful in dry arrangements.

Miscanthus sinensis 'Strictus' can also be known as porcupine grass and has a more erect habit than other *Miscanthus*. 'Zebrinus' or 'Zebra Grass' has mid-green leaves with yellow, broad, horizontal bands.

- Variegated grass with white margins on medium green leaves. Flowers emerge from the plant a bronze-red color and then turn a creamy color as the season wears on.
- Plant in a loose, moist soil with full sun.
- Blooms August to September.
- Height 5 feet.
- Propagate by division.

 *Resists deer.*

Cut Miscanthus down to the ground in the early spring so that the new foliage will not have to struggle up through last year's growth. Their dormant forms can be enjoyed through the winter. Lightly dusted with snow, they are at their beautiful winter best.

PAMPAS GRASS
(Cortaderia selloana)

The genus, *Cortaderia* is native to the grasslands of Argentina. In August, this ornamental grass bears thick stemmed plumes of gold, silver or rose-pink flowers. Try using the plumes in fresh or dried flower arrangements.

Pampas grass is relatively easy to grow. It performs quite well in dry, infertile soils but does its best with consistent moisture. Give young pampas grass plants a thick mulch during cold and windy winters.

There are some new variegated *Cortaderia* selections to try. 'Gold Band' has yellow margins on its leaves. 'Silver Stripe' or 'Albolineata' grows more slowly than other members of *Cortaderia* but does have attractive white margined leaves and silvery white plumes.

- Plants grow in dense tufts of evergreen, saw-toothed edged, arching leaves.
- Grow in full sun with an average, well-drained, moist soil.
- Blooms August to September.
- Height 8 to 10 feet. Very fast growing plant, can go from gallon size to 8 feet in one season. Can reach 20 feet if left alone.
- Propagate by division or seed.

SEA OATS, BAMBOO GRASS
(Chasmanthium latifolium)

The *Chasmanthium* genus contains about six species that are native to woodlands in Eastern and Central United States, Mexico and Central America. *C. latifolium* is the most widely cultivated and is sometimes listed as *Uniola latifolia*. Excellent for floral arrangements.

- Ornamental grass with broad, bamboo-like, light green leaves with arching stems. Changes to copper in fall and brown in winter.
- Grows in fertile, well-drained soil in full sun to part shade. Likes regular water.
- Stems carry silvery green flower spikelets that look like flattened oats. Seed heads are green when new and ripen to an attractive brown color.
- Height 3 to 5 feet.
- Propagate by division between mid-spring and early summer.

ASTER, MICHAELMAS DAISY
(Aster novi-belgii)

Aster novi-belgii is the actual name of hybrids that cross *A. novae-angliae* (New England Aster) and *A. novi-belgii* (New York Aster). Out of the more than 600 species of true asters, Michaelmas daisies are the last to bloom during the growing season. Pinch in late spring to produce more flowers and bushier growth. Some of the taller varieties may need staking in windier areas of the garden.

- Flower color magenta.
- Best in full sun and tolerates heat.
- Blooms May to October.
- Height 3 feet. Dwarf varieties available.
- Propagate by dividing clumps.

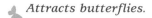 ***Attracts butterflies.***

ASTER, STOKES
(Stokesia laevis)

Native to South Carolina south to Louisiana and Florida.

- Flowers blue, lavender or white.
- Requires well-drained soil and full sun. Tolerates alkaline soil.
- Blooms June to September.
- Height 12 to 18 inches.
- Propagate from root cuttings, dividing in spring.

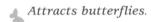LUEBEARD
(Caryopteris clandonensis)

Genus from Asia.

Several varieties of *C. Clandonesis* have gray or silver foliage. 'Dark Knight' and 'Longwood Blue' have silvery foliage. 'Worcester Gold' has yellow leaves. 'Blue Mist' has light blue flowers, while 'Dark Knight' and 'Heavenly Blue' have dark blue flowers.

- Bears tiny clusters of light blue to dark blue flowers on straight stems.
- Tolerates dry soils.
- Blooms August until frost.
- Height 2 to 4 feet.
- Propagate with cuttings.

🦋 *Attracts butterflies.*

Prune Bluebeards hard either in early winter or in the early spring before the new growth begins. The tops are prone to winter damage, especially in windy climates. Cut the plants back to within 2 to 4 inches of the ground. Bluebeards bloom on current years growth.

CHRYSANTHEMUM
(Chrysanthemum morifolium)

The *Chrysanthemum* genus contains about 160 species that are mostly native to China, Japan and Europe. *Chrysanthemum morifolium* can also be listed as *Dendranthema grandiflorum*. These are the mums that florists and nurseries commonly sell. They are the most useful and varied of all the *Chrysanthemum* species. Try them in pots, along borders or in a cutting garden.

Pinching encourages more flowers and bushiness. Start when spring growth is about 6 inches.

- Flower color yellow, red, pink, orange, purple, and bi-color.
- Grow in loose, fertile soil with full sun to part shade. Provide afternoon shade in hot climates.
- Blooms July to September.
- Height 8 inches to 2 feet.
- Propagate through softwood cuttings or by division.

CUSHION SPURGE
(Euphorbia epithymoides)

This native to Eastern Europe is also known as *E. polychroma*. It tolerates windy areas of the garden. This plant has a three-season interest. In spring, it takes on a bright yellow color, then it turns green and finally turns red in the fall.

Spurges contain sap that is highly irritating upon contact, especially to the eyes, mouth, and upon prolonged exposure to skin.

- Actual flowers are inconspicuous. The bracts of the plant are yellow.
- Plant in an average, well drained, loose soil that's not too wet.
- Blooms in September.
- Height 10 to 12 inches.
- Propagate with softwood cuttings.

Resists deer.

DUSTY MILLER
(Senecio cineraria)

Dusty Miller makes a good border plant. It is primarily grown for its silvery foliage which makes an interesting addition to fresh flower arrangements.

This plant is related to the daisy family, but Dusty Miller is also sold under the following Latin names: *Centaurea gymnocarpa*, *Centaurea cineraria*, *Chrysanthemum ptarmiciflorum* and *Senecio viravira*.

- Yellow, cream flowers.
- Tolerates dry soil and full sun.
- Blooms August to September.
- Height 12 to 18 inches.
- Propagate with cuttings.

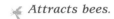 **Attracts bees.**

All plant parts of Senecio spp. *are poisonous, with higher concentrations in the seeds.*

GOLDENROD
(Solidago hybrids)

Goldenrod is a member of the daisy family. Parentage is uncertain, but goldenrod is probably from Europe and the Eastern United States. The plants can go for years without requiring division for rejuvenation. The growth habit is very restrained thus making it long-lived and never invasive. However, if the flower stalks are allowed to go to seed, goldenrod will self-sow freely and may become "weedy." *Solidago sempervirens* does not self-sow as readily as other members of goldenrod.

The flowers are suitable for fresh or dried arrangements and have a nice, subtle fragrance.

- Huge quantities of tiny flowers bloom on flat clusters that can range in shades of yellow from canary to dark gold. Leaves are medium-green and lance shaped.
- Plant in almost any type of moist soil in full sun.
- Blooms in August and September.
- Grows from 1-1/2 to 3-1/2 feet tall.
- Propagate by seed or division.

Contrary to popular opinion, goldenrod does not cause hayfever. It blooms the same time as ragweed (Ambrosia spp.). Goldenrod's pollen is heavy and waxy thus making it unsuitable to travel through the air.

*R*OSEMALLOW
(Hibiscus moscheutos)

Can also be commonly known as swamp mallow. Native to marshes in the Eastern United States. These large plants can bear blossoms that can reach one foot across. Since these large flowers can get rather heavy, make sure they have wind protection.

- Huge white or pink blooms.
- Plant in moist, average, well-drained soil in a sunny or partially shaded spot.
- Blooms late June until frost.
- Can grow from 4 to 8 feet tall.
- Propagate by division or by taking stem cuttings in the summer.

Attracts hummingbirds.

*R*USSIAN *S*AGE
(Perovskia atriplicifolia)

This native of Afghanistan has terrific attributes. It tolerates alkaline, dry soils. It even requires little water once established. Its semi-woody nature has silvery, aromatic foliage that opens 3 to 4 feet wide. However, it fares poorly in soggy soils and in shade. No wonder the Perennial Plant Association chose Russian Sage as the Perennial Plant of the Year for 1995!

- Small violet-blue flowers on 12 inch long stems.
- Plant in a well-drained soil of average fertility with full sun exposure.
- Blooms July through September.
- Height 4 feet.
- Propagate with softwood cuttings.

SEDUM
(Sedum spp.)

Groundcover varieties will not take foot traffic, the semi-succulent leaves crush easily. All Sedum species are nice, low maintenance plants.

S. spathulifolium is native from California's coastal regions and the Sierra Nevada mountains north to British Columbia.

SEDUM, STONE CROP
(Sedum spectabile)

Native to China and Japan. Flower clusters are excellent for dried arrangements, or leave the flowers to dry on the plant to create a winter interest.

* Flowers pink, red or white.
* Tolerates heat and dry soils and can tolerate some clay in the soil.
* Blooms July to August.
* Height 1 to 1-1/2 feet.
* Propagate with cuttings or by division.

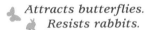 **Attracts butterflies.**
Resists rabbits.

SEDUM, DRAGON'S BLOOD
(Sedum spurium)

This evergreen plant makes a good ground cover.

* Bronze leaves and rosy red flowers.
* Tolerates heat and dry soils.
* Blooms in July.
* Height up to 6 inches.
* Propagate with cuttings or by division.

SEDUM, AUTUMN JOY
(Sedum telephium)

Resembles *S. spectabile* and provides four seasons of interest.

* Chocolate red flowers turn to large purple seed clusters.
* Tolerates heat and dry soils.
* Blooms in August.
* Height 2 to 2-1/2 feet.
* Propagate by taking leaf cuttings or by division.

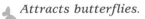 **Attracts butterflies.**

Index

Index

Bibliography

All About Perennials. San Ramon, CA.: Ortho Books, 1992.

Baldwin, Brian. "Sunflowers are all the rage." http://www.ag.usask.ca/cofa/departments/hort/hortinfo/yards/sunflowe.html. (11 Nov. 1997).

Blanchette, Leo. "Astilbes." Horticulture. June/July, 1997 p.59.

Day, Alice. "Gothic Gardening–Gothic Plant Tales." http://www.gothic.net/ ~ malice/gptindex.html. (11 Nov. 1997).

Eisenstein, Jessie. "Natural Healing." Flower & Garden. September, 1996 pp. 14-15.

Fischer, Thomas. "The Other Asters." Horticulture. October, 1997 pp. 36-40.

Grieve, Mrs. M. "Botanical.com A Modern Herbal." http://www.botanical.com/botanical/mgmh/h/helbla14.html. (11 Nov. 1997).

"Health Library–Pellitory." http://www.thriveonline.com/@@5*kyUAcAlEett6rx/thrive/health/Library/vitamins/vitamin219.html. (11 Nov. 1997).

Helmer, M. Jane Coleman, Ph.D. and Decker Hodge, Karla S., B.S. *Pictorial Guide to Perennials*. 2nd ed. Kalamazoo, MI.: Merchants Publishing, 1996.

Hermes, Alfred R. "A Wealth of Dianthus." Horticulture. May, 1997 pp. 39-42.

MacDougall, Dr. Maureen. "Indiana Plants Poisonous to Livestock and Pets." http://www.vet.purdue.edu/depts/addl/toxic/cover1.htm (11 Nov. 1997).

Mitchell, Lee. "Simply Sage." Flower & Garden. December, 1996 pp. 30-31.

"Native Wildflowers of the North Dakota Grasslands–Western Wallflower." http://www.npsc.nbs.gov/resource/literatr/wildflwr/species/erysaspe.htm. (11 Nov. 1997).

Rickert, R. "Jersualem Artichoke." http://holoweb.com/cannon/jerusale.htm. (11 Nov. 1997).

Rodale's Illustrated Encyclopedia of Gardening and Landscaping Techniques. Emmaus, PA.: Rodale Press, 1990.

Smith, Dr. Mary C. "Cornell University Poisonous Plants Web." http://www.ansci.cornell.edu/plants.html. (11 Nov. 1997).

Springer, Lauren. "A Parade of Poppies." Horticulture. June/July, 1997 pp. 41-46.

Sunset Western Garden Book. rev. ed. Menlo Park, CA.: Sunset Publishing, 1995.

The American Horticultural Society A-Z Encyclopedia of Garden Plants. New York.: DK Publishing, 1997.

The Columbia Dictionary of Quotations. New York.: Columbia University Press, 1995.

"The Mints of Texas–Physostegia." http://mahogany.lib.utexas.edu/Libs/LSL/Mints/physostegia/physostegia.html. (11 Nov. 1997).

Wagstaff, D. Jesse, DVM. "Checklist of Vascular Plants Reported to be Toxic." http://vm.cfsan.fda.gov/ ~ djw/plantnam.txt. (11 Nov. 1997).

Zona, Scott. "Botanical Nomenclature." Horticulture. May, 1996, p. 16.